THE EMPLOYMENT MAZE

Unlocking Doors To A New Job!

---

by Paul Dombroski

&

David Hage and Dennis Hage

DOUBLE TAKE BOOKS
PHOENIX

THE EMPLOYMENT MAZE
A Double Take Book

Statements in this book concerning contractual or legal issues are general statements. This book does not purport to be a substitute for the advice of an attorney in dealing with specific situations or problems that may confront the job applicant. This publication is designed to provide accurate and authoritive information in regard to the subject matter covered. It is sold with the understanding that the author or publisher is not engaged in rendering legal, accounting, or other professional service. If legal advice or other expert assistance is required, the services of a competent professional person should be sought.

PDQ Job Finding System is a trademark of Double Take Productions, Inc.
For information address: Double Take Productions, Inc.,
P.O. Box 26027, Phoenix, Az. 85068

Library of Congress Card Catalog Number: 89-50574

ISBN: 0-9622443-1-7

DOUBLE TAKE BOOKS ARE PUBLISHED BY DOUBLE TAKE PRODUCTIONS, INC.,

FIRST EDITION

PRINTED IN THE UNITED STATES OF AMERICA

Dedication

This book is dedicated to my wife, Tricia; my son, Jeffrey; and my daughter, Christina, who constantly encouraged me during the writing process. They sacrificed many hours of quality family time so I could concentrate on this project. Most importantly, it is right to give thanks and praise to the good Lord, whose spiritual inspiration and guidance allowed me to fulfill my dream of writing this book.

Acknowledgements

Thanks to: Ric Napoli and Tom O'Connell for their great illustrations; and Jim Sullivan, Dick Hoover, Wayne Steele, Virginia, Pamela, and Joseph Hage for their comments and proof reading. A special thanks to David and Dennis Hage, who spent countless hours editing, rewriting, and adding many new and creative ideas to this book. Without their help, it would never have materialized.

Table of Contents

Door 5 – Outside Help
Grouping in the Dark

Door 6 – The Interview
The "Route" of the Problem

Door 7 – Negotiation
Let's Make a Deal

Closing the Door – Out of the Maze

OPENING THE DOOR

The Labyrinth ... Preface to the Maze

PDQ 101 ... An Introduction

OPENING THE DOOR

THE LABYRINTH

Preface to the Maze

In a flash, another memory came to him, something he had been told when he was about twelve, a method for finding one's way out of any maze. It was simple, and it was effective—he had tried it several times and lost all interest in mazes thereafter because it had taken away the challenge. All you had to do, he recalled, was to keep your hand—or your pencil—on one wall, the left-hand wall, let us say. However far it took you, you were never to remove your hand from it, and in the end, even though you went into every dead end and crossed your own tracks several times, you would emerge from the maze.

—DANIEL EASTERMAN
The Seventh Sanctuary, 1987

To the first time job seeker and even the seasoned professional there seems to be an inordinate amount of information regarding the correct methods to gain employment. This data overload has led many into a maze of confusion. Not knowing what to do, many job seekers have wasted thousands of hours and dollars wandering down empty corridors. Quickly finding your way through the employment maze to a new and better job is the subject that is addressed in the upcoming chapters.

Every year, millions of people in this country spend an enormous quantity of time and money in an attempt to find the ideal job. They seek help from friends, professional associates, or anyone else that promises rapid success in their job search endeavors. In addition, a vast number of unknowledge-able job hunters succumb to the false hopes that are often portrayed by so-called professional job hunting service firms. Even though most service firms are very reputable, the job seeker is not able to separate fact from fiction when dealing with an unscrupulous vendor.

Knowledge is the key in making a successful decision about your career. A lack of it can be very costly when it comes to job hunting. This book should impart to you the distinctive elements that comprise a successful job search. You will develop a keen sense of direction on how to proceed through the maze.

As you read through the book, watch for **Key Points.** These denote special emphasis of the topic under discussion and are essential elements in the entire job hunting process. Each of these Key Points will add to your overall success in landing a new job. Many are techniques that are extremely effective, but not necessarily widely known.

Key Point Establish a good filing and tracking system. Expand the file information as you make progress. Set up a checklist of tasks that need to be accomplished. Establish specific goals and timetables. If you have a home computer, start a data base file of job hunting activities. Keep all contact information in the data base for future referral.

Keep an open mind and be ready to absorb new ideas. Write down thoughts immediately, as they surface. Space is provided throughout the book for notes. The mind should be stimulated and many questions will come forth regarding the principles presented. Creative thinking unfolds the responses to various questions posed. These thoughts assist in the strategic planning process necessary in a job search.

PDQ 101
An Introduction

Directly opposite him, on the other side of the enclosed space, were two doors, exactly alike and side by side.... If he opened the one, there came out of it a hungry tiger.... But if the accused person opened the other door, there came forth a lady, the most suitable to his years and station.... Without the slightest hesitation, he went to the door on the right and opened it.

–FRANK STOCKTON
The Lady or the Tiger, 1884

My last twenty years in the personnel and human relations field have provided the opportunity to review thousands of resumes and interview almost as many applicants. During this period, nearly every method imaginable has been tried to attract my attention. Some of the more creative approaches range from a cartoon resume that utilized the B.C. comic strip character to a narrative resume on a small, flexible, plastic record. While these novel approaches captured my interest, they were not effective in achieving the ultimate objective, the interview and subsequent job offer.

There are pros and cons about the various ways recommended to find a new job. I decided it was time to assimilate the wealth of existing knowledge into a **simplified** job hunting plan from the perspective of the hiring manager. My goal in writing this book is to expose the reader to the tools and methods that should be used in conducting a search for a new job, many of which are not known to the average person. My co-authors and marketing consultants on this book, David and Dennis Hage, created the name for these techniques – The PDQ Job Finding System. No, PDQ doesn't stand for **P**retty "**D**arn" **Q**uick, it is an acronym for **P**aul **D**ombroski's **Q**uick Job Finding System.

A quick example of the PDQ system is in where to look for jobs. Most people start their search in the newspaper. You may ask, "What's wrong with that?" Well, on the surface, nothing. But think, how many jobs have you landed using want ads? Up to this point in my career, I have never received a job offer that resulted from a response to a want ad in the newspaper. If the job seeker depends on ads as the sole method to secure a new job, he or she may be on the job market for a long time. As you progress through this book, you will begin to understand the necessity to go beyond the want ads.

Key Point Most job openings are not advertised. It is estimated that the published want ads represent only 15 to 25% of the current, professional-level job openings. That means that 75 to 85% of professional jobs are filled by people who utilize other methods. To be successful in a job search you must do more than just send a resume to the companies that advertise in the newspaper.

Many books have been written on how to find a job. These books range in emphasis from the creation of a "super resume" to working with "head-hunters." Each author offers segmented information as it relates to the entire job hunting process. I do not take a fragmented approach and only examine one or two facets of a job search. Rather, I present a complete and systematic approach to a successful job change, i.e., the PDQ Job Finding System.

This book is not intended to make you an overnight expert in hiring practices. Only years of experience in recruitment and placement makes one proficient in this area. Rather, the information presented should create an awareness of the job hunting methods that are available for use by the prospective job hunter.

In essence, the material presented enables the formulation of a strategy to market oneself in the business world. Yes, that's right. Market yourself just as a company would market a product or service. An example that comes to mind is the story told by Harry Reichenbach, the "Father of Ballyhoo," about Francis X. Bushman, a small-time, $250 a week actor in Chicago:

> "I wanted to raise his salary to a commanding figure. When we arrived in New York I had 2,000 pennies in my pocket. As we walked along 42nd Street toward the Metro office, I dropped handfuls of pennies in our line of march. At first children followed to pick up the coins, then everybody followed. By the time we reached Metro the streets were black with milling crowds.... When the officers of Metro looked out of the window, they judged Bushman's popularity

> by the vast throngs that had followed us and he received $1,000 a week without any argument."

Each person has a wealth of knowledge and experience that is needed in many companies. I will teach you how to "package" and market your expertise. This is discussed later as my "value" concept. A careful review of my PDQ system provides the keys to "unlock the doors through the employment maze" and significantly increase the probability of obtaining that new position.

DOOR 1

LOST IN THE MAZE

The Start ... Or Finished?

Mirrors in the Maze ... or
Take a Close Look at Yourself

Ready ... Set, Goals

Rank and File ... Your Priorities

"Move it or Lose it" ... or Relocation Choices

DOOR 1

LOST IN THE MAZE
The Start ... Or Finished?

They finally awoke to black night. Hansel comforted his little sister, saying, "Just wait until the moon comes up, Gretel. Then we'll see the breadcrumbs I dropped, and they'll show us the way home."

When the moon appeared, they got up. But the breadcrumbs were gone, for the many thousands of birds of the field and forest had picked them all up.

"We will find the way all the same," said Hansel to Gretel, but they did not. They walked the whole night and the next day from morning till evening, but they did not come out of the forest.

—THE BROTHERS GRIMM
Hansel and Gretel, Circa 1820

Your search for a new job should begin with an examination of several critical topics. Each one of these areas has a significant impact on the direction you choose to take. A careful review of priorities, goals, relocation, and types of organizations is essential before a course of action can be established.

Mirrors in the Maze ... or Take a Close Look at Yourself

Mirror, mirror, on the wall, who's the fairest of them all?

—THE EVIL QUEEN
Snow White and the Seven Dwarfs

The first step on the path to a successful job search should be an analysis of your needs and values. By initiating a self-evaluation, answers to your personal and career questions become evident. You will be in a better position to set realistic life goals and establish an action plan. While the process sometimes seems like a "House of Mirrors," keep looking and soon you will find the real you in the reflection.

What makes a person desire to change jobs? Keep this question and thought in mind while I address a major problem, i.e., a lack of self-direction. Talking to thousands of applicants over the years has brought a very serious fact to my attention. Many people who are dissatisfied with their jobs have problems that extend far beyond what they discuss or ever admit to themselves. Changing jobs won't necessarily make things better! By understanding your motivation, a specific course of action can be formulated to achieve the results in the job hunting process.

I have categorized three types of individuals who are negatively motivated to change jobs. I call them the "Wanderers, Groaners, and Talkers." As you read through the description of each, see if any of the characteristics are applicable to your situation.

Do you know someone who has roamed aimlessly from one company to another, changing jobs every year or so? I call these people "The Wanderers." They have no idea what career direction to take or what to expect from their company. These Wanderers cannot give a logical rationale for a job change. They blame the boss, co-workers, or whoever seems to fit the circumstances. The Wanderers always think the grass will be greener working for someone else.

Then there are "The Groaners," who complain about everything. They criticize everyone in the company and always have a better way of doing someone else's job. An aura of negativity surrounds them. If their company puts on a Christmas dinner party for the employees, there are complaints about the free food. These are the people who go through the same routine every week – they gripe while at work, wait for the weekend and then dread the return to work Monday morning. There is no focus on personal goals or objectives, let alone business ones.

The last group is "The Talkers." The Talker always says a job change is under consideration, but never takes any action to start the process. I know one individual who told me he was going to change jobs. In fact, he has been telling me the same story for the last 10 years. The Talkers constantly discuss the possibility of a job change, but lack either the ambition or knowledge of which direction to go in the maze. They short change themselves by not actively looking at potential opportunities for further growth and development.

Are any of these descriptions of the Wanderer, Groaner, or Talker characteristic of your behavior? If so, take heed. These kinds of individuals wind up at a dead end as they make their way through the employment maze. Evaluate what motivates you and ask, "Do I really know what I want out of life?" Once you begin to understand what your needs are, the process of establishing realistic life goals will unfold.

You still have to fill out the application form, Mr. Rambo!

A Double Take Cartoon

Ready ... Set, Goals

The most successful business man is the man who holds on to the old just as long as it is good and grabs the new just as it is better.

—ROBERT P. VANDERPOEL

By this point, a number of questions should be going through your mind. Do I fit into one of the three categories discussed (Wanderers, Groaners, Talkers)? If so, how did I get there? What can I do about it? By making an honest assessment you are in a better position to set realistic life goals. Keep in mind that the establishment of goals is essential before career options can effectively be determined. Think about the answers to the following set of questions:

- What do I want out of life?
- How am I going to get there?
- How are the relationships in my family?
- What about my social needs?
- What do I want out of a job?
- Do I value any unique type of recreational activity?
- Is a special type of community important to me?
- What about my spiritual well-being?
- What are my short and long-term priorities?

The last question usually is the most revealing. Consider your answers and write several life goal statements. For example, I want to:

- attain the level of Vice President before I reach age 45.
- own and operate a business.
- become financially independent before age 65.
- retire by age 60.
- return to school and complete my college education.

- have sufficient financial resources to put my children through college.
- publish a book or set of articles.

LIFE GOAL STATEMENTS

If you are married, share these goals with your spouse. Single people should discuss their list with a close family member or friend. Evaluate the goal statements and determine if they are realistic, then go for it!

A goal-setting exercise may reveal that you have been going in the wrong direction for many years and have gained little ground, like wandering aimlessly through a life-size maze. Conversely, several areas may be identified that just need a sharper focus to put you back on the right path. Once you know what is important to achieve in your life, it becomes an easier task to find and implement the necessary strategies to make it happen.

Rank and File ... Your Priorities

We grow great by dreams. All big men are dreamers.... Some of us let these great dreams die, but others nourish and protect them; nurse them through bad days till they bring them to the sunshine and light, which comes always to those who sincerely hope that their dreams will come true.

—WOODROW WILSON

During the course of my career, I have asked friends and employees about their priorities in life. I was curious as to what order they ranked God, spouse, children, job, leisure, etc. A significant number responded that their job was number one on the list. It was also of interest to find that a significantly higher rate of family troubles were experienced by those who were married and ranked their jobs as number one. Likewise, single people who listed their job as number one showed a significant decrease in their social life and outside activities. Is there some correlation? Perhaps – just some food for thought.

After you decide what to achieve in life, a job can be one of the tools to help attain the goals. By selecting the best opportunity and being associated with the right company, a significantly higher degree of satisfaction with life in general may be experienced. Who knows, by going through this exercise you may find that a job change is not in order.

No matter how well we plan our lives or set goals, situations arise that are beyond our control. If, for example, a company goes through a merger or acquisition, it is certain that jobs will be consolidated or eliminated. A company may experience financial problems and have to downsize by laying off employees. Reorganizations can narrow the scope and opportunities for an individual, resulting in decreased job satisfaction. Working for a less than effective boss can also cause a great deal of frustration.

Every person should be aware of these factors. The odds are overwhelming that one of these situations will affect you sometime in your career. If you find yourself in one of these unfortunate circumstances, do not despair. Remember, there are always warning signs that precede these events. So pay attention, and you will have ample time to prepare for a possible job change. A temporary setback should not preclude anyone from attaining goals, but should be viewed as an opportunity to redefine the necessary action required to return to the right door of the maze.

"Move it or Lose it" ... or Relocation Choices

With these changes in latitudes, changes in attitudes,
nothing remains quite the same.
With all of our running, and all of our cunning,
if we couldn't laugh, we would all go insane.

–JIMMY BUFFET
Changes in Latitudes, Changes in Attitudes

After you complete the self-evaluation process and decide to make a career move, consider another significant factor. Ask yourself several basic questions. "Am I willing to relocate to another city? What about another state?" These should be the first series of potential problems contemplated prior to starting the actual job hunting process. A significant amount of time and effort will be wasted unless these are addressed. Experience has shown that relocation should be discussed with family members. Questions to ponder are:

1. If in a dual-income family, what impact will relocation have on the financial situation?

2. Is my spouse willing to move?

3. How do the children feel about moving away from familiar surroundings and their friends? Do I really want to take the kids out of school, especially if they only have one year left before graduation?

4. What about other relatives living in the immediate area?

5. Do I want to start over again in a new location?

6. Will I be able to adjust to climate changes? If living in San Diego, how easy will it be to acclimate to Chicago?

These are only a few of the basic questions that must be examined. Each person has a unique situation. You may be surprised at the support of family members willing to relocate. The excitement and adventure associated with a move to a new city can be a unifying and rewarding experience for the entire family.

Any relocation decision that affects family members must be made with considerable consultation and discussion. If the search is limited to a specific geographic area, it usually takes a longer time to find a new job.

Many job offers are turned down because of a relocation problem. This may be due to a lack of previous discussion and failure to plan with family members. Don't waste everyone's time, talk it over first! While there may be less of an impact for a single person, similar questions must be examined. By eliminating a possible problem, you will have successfully navigated another corridor in the employment maze.

NOTES ON RELOCATION:

Inter"lock"ing Directorates ... or "Pick" the Right Type of Company

I owe my soul to the company store.

TENNESSEE ERNIE FORD
From the song Sixteen Tons

The type of company selected to work for should not be taken lightly. A variety of corporate cultures exist and are unique in every organization. Before making a decision to join a business firm, determine the feasibility of attaining personal and professional goals within the constraints imposed by each organization under consideration.

I have had the opportunity to work for different sizes and types of companies. While there may be many variations, I have categorized these organizations and will discuss them briefly as follows:

- Small/Large
- Growth/Mature

I was admired and feared, but I was not royalty. And those people had more respect for royalty and nobility than for brains and talent. I could have got a title easily. But I didn't ask for it. I couldn't have felt fine and proud about any title except one that should come from the nation itself. In the course of years, I did win one. It fell from the lips of a blacksmith, and I liked it. It later became as familiar as the King's name. I was never known by any other name afterward. This title, in modern speech, was THE BOSS.

–MARK TWAIN
A Connecticul Yankee in King Arthur's Court

SMALL COMPANIES

Small businesses offer a significant amount of freedom and flexibility. However, less structure and a lack of uniform procedures can cause inconsistency in their operations. You may have to deal with an entrepreneur who started the firm and wants to run things one way. I recall a small company that was on its way to success. Sales increased 30% per year and the owner sought key professionals throughout the country to join the organization. Due to the rapid growth rate and profitability, the firm was able to attract very talented executives. The company went public and the stock value soared. Yet within a period of three years, the price of the company's stock fell dramatically and all the key people left.

So what happened and why is it important to our discussion? Very simply, the owner would not release control to the expert staff that was assembled. His archaic management style was forced throughout the organization. This created a severe morale problem that resulted in massive managerial turnover. Therefore, if you consider a small company, be sure to check it out thoroughly. Find out as much as possible about the management style and mode of operation.

Small Company Advantages	Small Company Disadvantages
High degree of freedom	Lack of policies and procedures
Significant flexibility	Unstructured
Broad based responsibility	Inconsistencies
More visibility and faster recognition	Entrepreneur style of management
Quick promotions	Insufficient financial resources

LARGE COMPANIES

Large companies offer a more structured, regimented environment. Jobs are very focused and usually have formalized descriptions. There is less freedom to act without numerous committee meetings and obtaining several levels of approvals. This well-defined type of environment may be very attractive to some individuals and viewed as less threatening than that of a small company.

I know many people who get frustrated working in a large company. The entrepreneurs just don't like having to deal with twenty people in a week-long committee meeting to discuss the color of a knob. These "free spirits" soon get the urge to change jobs or become very discouraged in their jobs.

Large Company Advantages	Large Company Disadvantages
Highly structured	Less freedom to act independently
More resources	Committee decisions
Very focused jobs	Length of time to accomplish tasks
Good benefits	Low visibility

Big Boss Man, can't you hear me when I call,
you ain't so big, you're tall, that's all.
Well I'm gonna get a boss man, one that treats me right,
work hard in the day, resting in the night.

–ELVIS
Big Boss Man
Al Smith and Luther Dixon

GROWTH COMPANIES

Growth companies naturally start small and have the potential of substantial expansion. Carefully examine the type of service or product offered and the particular industry. A business that grows too fast may be focused in a very narrow market and success short lived. If you are convinced that the company under evaluation has exceptional potential, the following incident should be taken into consideration.

A good friend of mine accepted a position in a growth firm, but soon came to some startling realities. He found himself taking on additional areas of responsibility without adequate resources to do an effective job. An enormous amount of time and energy was spent in order to perform his work. After two years of 60 hour weeks and no time for a vacation, he was burned out. Was it worth it? While he gained more experience in those two years than he would have in five years in a more stable company, he could not attain the level of self-satisfaction desired and subsequently sought out another firm.

On the positive side, growth companies offer substantial freedom to act, fast promotional potential, and the opportunity for equity participation. Consider your personality and decide if you want to work in this type of environment.

Growth Company Advantages	Growth Company Disadvantages
Rapid expansion	Business plans change frequently
Wide variance in job responsibilities	Priorities change constantly
Fast implementation of decisions	Lack of people to fill vacancies
High visibility	Long work hours
Quick financial rewards	High degree of stress

MATURE COMPANIES

The mature organization that grows at a modest 10 to 15% a year with a reasonable return on investment can be another attractive place to seek employment. The problem, however, may be in getting the job. These companies are usually very stable and have a low turnover rate. Employees often enjoy the environment and generally have a longer tenure. If they perform adequately, the mature company provides the highest degree of security.

Mature Company Advantages	Mature Company Disadvantages
Very stable, low turnover	Large resistance to change
Well defined jobs	Complacency
Positive work environment	Lack of growth opportunities
Financial security	Employees become internalized

CAUTION

SWINGING DOOR!

A note of caution, complacency may settle into mature organizations over a period of time and could have an adverse impact on performance. Additionally, people may become internalized. They do things only one way, "the company way." The drawback is that these individuals become less marketable over time. If someone has spent the first 15+ years of a career in a single company and only has one base of experience to draw from, another firm may be hesitant to hire that person. Companies often want employees with significant breadth and depth of experience drawn from different organizations, not just one. The days of spending a lifetime with one company are over. Additionally, it is probable that the individual is in a very good financial position, which makes the decision to change jobs more difficult.

While there are many other examples and variations of company size and composition, an awareness of general characteristics should be carefully examined and considered before a specific one is selected. Each type of organization mentioned has advantages and disadvantages. Examine each and determine which best suits your goals. William S. Knudsen had these words to offer: "A big corporation is more or less blamed for being big; it is only big because it gives service. If it doesn't give service, it gets small faster than it grew."

Take this job and shove it, I ain't working here no more.
My woman done left and took all the reasons I was working for.
You better not try to stand in my way, cause I'm walking out the door.
Take this job and shove it, I ain't working here no more.

–JOHNY PAYCHECK
From the song by David Allen Coe

Revolving Doors ... A Review

To summarize the PDQ system to this point, the first step on the path to a new job is a self-examination and the setting of life goals. Analyze your current job and family situation. Set realistic goals and start to formulate a strategy on how they can be achieved. If your current position is not on the right path towards an established goal, then a job hunting strategy must be developed. Evaluate the type of organization that fits into your life. Then, to avoid potential problems discuss the possibility of making a change with the family. After the decision is made to find a new job, you need to know how to identify new career possibilities. The next stop through the employment maze provides directions on where to find those hidden opportunities.

DOOR 2

THE PDQ NETWORK

How to Win (with) Friends and Influence People

How Does the Net Work? ... or
The ABC's of Networks

Trust or Consequences ... or
Preparing a List

"A Maze" Your Friends!
Go See Them – It Pays

Put Your Foot in the Door ... or
Using Your Networkers' Info

DOOR 2

THE PDQ NETWORK

How to Win (with) Friends and Influence People

Tomorrow you will want to persuade somebody to do something. Before you speak, pause and ask: "How can I make him want to do it?" ... I have discovered from personal experience that one can win the attention and time and co-operation of even the most sought after people in America by becoming genuinely interested in them.

–DALE CARNEGIE

Entering Door number 2, you should already have made several significant decisions about a job change. The next logical question you should ask is, "Where do I go from here?" The answer is to establish a network. It will allow you to develop vital sources of information about the hidden job market. With the use of referrals, telephone calls, advertisements, and a direct mail campaign, a number of key opportunities will begin to surface and you will see how to use your network.

How Does the Net Work? ... or The ABC's of Networks

Certainly it takes more work for a station which does not rely on a network. It is far easier to patch in the network...

—FRANK STANTON, President of CBS
From the book The Networks

As previously mentioned, 75 to 85% of the available professional jobs are never advertised. We next explore several methods that can be utilized to seek out those hidden opportunities and open the door to an interview.

Everyone is familiar with the national television networks. ABC, CBS, and NBC all have affiliate stations throughout the country that broadcast similar programs. The purpose of these networks is to gather and provide visual information and entertainment. Television networks also share information with each other in order to provide the broadest news coverage to the public. Likewise, a network in a job search is similar, i.e., provide information about potential opportunities to people who share common goals and who work as a team. "Networkers" is the word David & Dennis Hage, my marketing consultants, coined to describe the group that you will select to help you.

By the simple utilization of personal and professional contacts (Networkers), information about job opportunities and availability can be gathered and acted upon.

A Double Take Cartoon

Trust or Consequences ... or Preparing a List

Mention not a rope in the house of one whose father was hanged.

–OLD PROVERB

The King, a man fond of games and riddles, posed this one to the bandit: "You may make one statement. If you tell the truth in it, you will be shot. If you lie, you will be hanged." The bandit put everything in a fine mess with this reply: – "I am going to be hanged."

–G. K. CHESTERTON

In the PDQ network approach to a job search, trust in your Networkers is of paramount importance. There are potential risks involved with the use of a network. If complete confidence is placed in a person who is not trustworthy, everyone in town (including the boss) may know you are looking for a job. Keep this in mind when you assess the value each Networker can bring to the job search efforts.

The types of Networkers should range from personal friends to professional associates. For example, assume you are the buyer for an electronics firm and decide to move to another job. Research is conducted, personal and professional goals are set, and the conclusion is reached that a job search is mandatory. Next you ask, "How do I establish my network?" The first step is to brainstorm – list all associates who might become Networkers and help you in a job search. For example:

NAME	PHONE	OCCUPATION	TRUST	RANK
Bill Williams	555-1111	Sr. Buyer at XYZ Corp	Excellent	10
Paul Wilson	555-2222	Purchasing Manager	Fair	8
Phil Adams	555-3333	Manufacturer Rep	Poor	5
Fred Jones	555-1212	Buyer at ABC Electric	Good	6
Susan Smith	555-4444	Buyer at M.S.Supply	Excellent	9

Before reading further take a minute or two and write down a few names to include in your PDQ Networker list.

PDQ NETWORKER LIST

NAME	PHONE	OCCUPATION	TRUST	RANK

Get the Idea? This list can be expanded to include as many names as necessary. Think of all those vendors who call. What about the people you met at the buyer's convention last month? Pull out their business cards and jot down the names. Include non-business associates: friends, former classmates, doctors, lawyers, bankers, social club members, and church members. Finally, choose the best 15 to 25 people who will make a contribution to your efforts. Be honest in the evaluation of trust level.

CAUTION SWINGING DOOR!

Do not rank a person as a "10" just because he/she has a senior position in a company. This contact might know your boss and communicate back that you are looking for a new job. Be careful and objective in your selections.

"A Maze" Your Friends! Go See Them – It Pays

After reflection and planning comes the go or no-go decision. This is the stage, I believe, at which most objects falter. Anyone can reflect. Anyone can plan. The crunch comes with the move from thought to action, a giant step that requires energy, resolve, and a willingness to accept change.

–LAWRENCE SANDERS
The Tomorrow File

Contact your PDQ Networkers by telephone. Explain that you are planning a career move and are confident they can help in the endeavor. Request a meeting at lunch, after work, on the tennis court, or golf course. At the designated meeting, provide specific background and skills information. Tell them about the types of positions and companies in which there is interest. Ask for assistance in making contacts with people in their organization or another company where they may know of a job opening. It is amazing how many people are aware of either current openings or upcoming opportunities that have not been released to the personnel department for recruitment.

Do not leave the meeting without the names of at least 3 to 5 people who can be contacted. It is of vital importance to obtain these names in order to effectively use a network. It is really a number's game. The more quality people that make up a network, the better the odds are of hitting the jackpot, i.e., a job opportunity. The network should be considered successful if 15 meetings are held and three referrals are obtained from each Networker. Once again, make sure members of your network understand the need for confidentiality and discretion.

Use the names of friends and business associates to make initial contact with potential employers. This referral type of "door opener" is one of the best ways to use your network.

Put Your Foot in the Door ... or Using Your Networkers' Info

"It is I!"
"Who is I?"
"Pinocchio."
"Ah, I understand!" said the Snail. "Wait for me there. I will come down and open the door directly."
An hour passed, and then two, and the door was not opened.... And drawing back he gave a tremendous kick against the house door. The blow was indeed so violent that his foot went through the wood and stuck...

–CARLO COLLODI
The Adventures Of Pinocchio, 1880

To make it through any maze quickly, do not get detoured or stuck along the way. These next sections discuss three approaches to directly gain access to the hiring or high-level manager's door using your PDQ network.

Let us go back to the network list example. Bill Williams, the senior buyer from XYZ Corporation, gives you the name of Tom Thompson, Purchasing Manager at another company. Tom had mentioned to Bill at a purchasing association luncheon that a position would soon open for a senior buyer. Now that you have a solid lead, what next? Call your lead, in this case Mr. Thompson.

Try my PDQ "After Five" telephone approach and call just after closing time. Managers are usually still at work and more likely to answer their own telephone. This technique reduces the risk of being screened out by a secretary.

So it is 5:30 P.M. and you call Mr. Thompson, who picks up the phone. The conversation should go something like this:

> *Mr. Thompson:* "Hello, this is Tom Thompson.".
>
> *Caller:* "Hello Mr. Thompson, this is _______. I am the buyer at Liberty Bell Electronics. I was meeting with a mutual acquaintance, Bill Williams, the senior buyer at XYZ Corporation, the other day. Bill mentioned a conversation he had with you regarding a possible opening for a senior buyer at your company. I would like to make you aware of my interest in that position."

This initial telephone call is the most significant event that could lead to a face-to-face interview. Be prepared to give a brief personal background emphasizing major achievements. Have a list of discussion topics in hand when you make the call. Convey enough information to whet the appetite and encourage a request for your resume and a meeting. Remember, when marketing yourself over the telephone, the interviewer must be convinced that a meeting would be beneficial.

Another PDQ network approach is to send letters to the people identified in the network process. Using the same analogy from our previous telephone approach, an introduction letter should read similiar to the example on the next page.

Network Introduction Letter Example

Dear Mr. Thompson:

At a recent meeting I had the opportunity to speak with Mr. Bill Williams, the senior buyer at XYZ Corporation. Mr. Williams informed me that during last month's purchasing association luncheon, he spoke with you and learned of an opening in your organization for a senior buyer. Briefly, I would like to express my interest in that position and present an outline of my qualifications.

In my present position as buyer at Liberty Bell Electronics, I have full responsibility of order placement with annual expenditures of $5 million dollars.

Several of my major accomplishments include:

Developed computerized purchasing order system

Reduced vendor delivery time to meet our "just in time" schedules

Documented cost savings of $500,000 in first year

Trained new expediters in policies and procedures.

At 30 years of age, I hold a BA degree with emphasis in purchasing from California State University. I am married with one child.

Confident that a personal discussion of the expertise I can offer your firm would be mutually beneficial, I would appreciate the opportunity for a personal interview. I will call in a few days to arrange for a meeting.

Sincerely yours,

Jeff Jones

What has been accomplished?

- An introduction was made using a referral.
- You conveyed an awareness of the opening.
- Career highlights, as they pertained to the position, were presented.
- A level of interest was created that generates further action.

A few days after the letter has been sent, follow up with a telephone call. Try to set up an interview with the manager. If the manager is unavailable, discuss with the secretary the possibility of a meeting. Secretaries can become your allies. If the name is not already known, ask the receptionist or telephone operator. Break the ice and try to win their confidence. It is surprising how cooperative they are when asked to check the boss' schedule to set up an appointment. I have seen many hiring managers consult with secretaries as to their opinion of the applicants. Making a good impression with an assistant never hurts the cause and may be the right combination to get your foot in the door!

A company's internal posting bulletin board is an additional source of potential job opportunities. Most firms post job openings in a location accessible to employees. Ask your Networkers to check at their companies.

If successful in obtaining an interview, but an offer does not materialize, make an effort to secure a referral from the hiring manager that conducted the interview — not the personnel people, as they usually just send out a nice "thank you" form letter. Place the new names received into the networking system for future use.

Once settled in a new job, it never hurts to follow up and let selected managers know where you are located. You may meet them someday at a professional association meeting or luncheon. Future opportunities may be knocking on your door, but you need to be listening.

Revolving Doors ... A Review

The establishment and implementation of a personal network is imperative to a successful job search. Do not underestimate the role networking plays in the job hunt process. Networking accounts for the majority of new professional job offers. Without its use, you will be walking down a potential dead-end corridor in the employment maze.

DOOR 3

HELP WANTED

Do You "Want Ads" To Work For You?

This Ad's for You? ... or Open Ads

RSVP (ReSpond Very Promptly) ... or Timing the Response

Follow(n) Up Again? Make Sure You Do!

Seeing Through ... Blind Ads

Out of ... "Position-Wanted" Ads

Check ... Lists and Directories

DOOR 3

HELP WANTED

Do You "Want Ads" To Work For You?

Everyone has his superstitions. One of mine has always been when I started to go anywhere, or to do anything, never to turn back or to stop until the thing was accomplished.

–ULYSSES S. GRANT

The first place people typically look when they start a campaign to find a new job is in the Sunday newspaper. Several large advertisements placed by major companies can be seen immediately. These "Open Ads" represent approximately 40% of published ads for professional positions. Also noticeable are ads with no company name, but with only a P.O. Box number as the return address. These are "Blind Ads" and make up the other 60% of those published for professional positions. Both of these types of recruitment advertisements will be discussed in this chapter.

This Ad's for You? ... or Open Ads

Alice went timidly up to the door and knocked.
"There's no sort of use in knocking," said the Footman, "and that for two reasons. First, because I'm on the same side of the door as you are. Secondly, because they're making such a noise inside that no one could possibly hear you."
"Please, then," said Alice, "how am I to get in?"
"There might be some sense in your knocking," the Footman went on, "if we had the door between us. For instance, if you were inside, you might knock, and I could let you out, you know."
"How am I to get in?" asked Alice again, louder.
"Are you to get in at all?" said the Footman." That's the first question, you know."
It was, no doubt – only Alice did not like to be told so.

–LEWIS CARROLL
Alice in Wonderland

Open ads placed by major companies in the local paper are usually for positions available in a very specific geographic area and represent jobs that are below $50,000 in annual salary. However, in large metropolitan areas it is common to find a company with an open position, in Chicago, for example, placing an advertisement in the New York Times. People in the larger population centers seem to be more mobile and would therefore be attracted by job opportunities in other major cities. This type of advertisement philosophy and practice occurs in most cities across the country.

Want ads are usually placed by the company personnel department's staff. Recruiters review the job specifications with management and then formulate the ad copy. Most personnel recruiters "shoot for the moon" with the requirements published in help wanted ads. They tend to overstate the experience and skills necessary for the position, knowing full well that the perfect candidate probably won't respond. This practice attempts to screen out the "deadwood." Many job seekers read the ad and think, "I guess I don't qualify, the requirements are too stiff." Don't be intimidated!

Recruiters seldom find a person meeting more than 75% of the stated requirements. Do not disqualify yourself! If your experience is anywhere close to the requirements, send a resume and cover letter.

Become familiar with your local newspaper. If there is more than one in town, the largest probably has a higher number of want ads and more opportunities. Companies placing ads review circulation numbers very closely and their advertising agencies keep them informed of any changes that may affect the recruitment campaign. Although most advertisements are placed in the Sunday newspapers, a few exceptions do exist. For example, the Wall Street Journal's heavy days for want ads are Tuesday and Wednesday. (See the Appendix for a list of major newspapers and their circulation.)

Also become very familiar with the industry trade journals, especially the high-tech ones, if you are a technical person. Companies often advertise in these types of magazines because they know that the readers' profile should match with the kind of employees they need. In the electronic's world alone, almost all of the weekly tabloids have a section for help wanted, and one specifically goes after this market, i.e., EDN Career News, which has a readership well over 100,000! Other major high-tech publications are Electronic Design, which has a monthly feature on the job market and EE Times, where the readers often look at the want ads before reading anything else. Trade publications may come out weekly or monthly and these ads are usually submitted weeks in advance of the publishing date.

A Double Take Cartoon

RSVP (ReSpond Very Promptly) ... or Timing the Response

Ya gotta send 'em to get 'em.

—RADAR O'REILLY
MASH Mail Call, 1981

The number of people who respond to want ads varies from region to region. I have placed hundreds of advertisements and the responses normally follow the traditional bell curve. Let us take a closer look at an example. A company places an advertisement in the local Sunday newspaper for a Director of Finance. The ad is "open" with full disclosure as to the company and location. A company typically receives 250 to 300 responses, sometimes even more. The response pattern would look something like this:

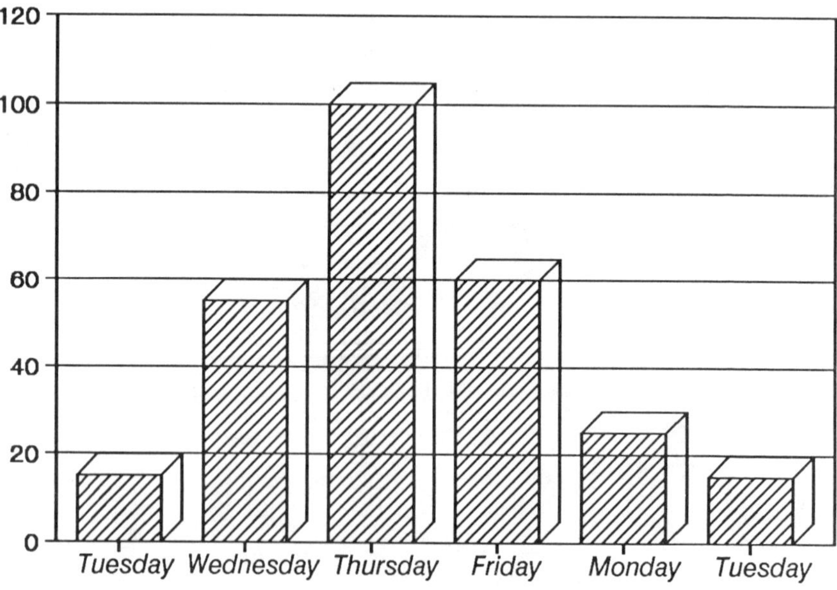

Opinions differ as to when one should respond to an ad. If a resume is sent too soon, the resume may get lost in the paper shuffle. However, if you wait too long, the door may close on opportunities.

When applying for a job with an estimated salary below $50,000, send in a resume a day or two after the ad was placed. This pays the best dividends. Recruiters may select just a few resumes to review and pick out three or four candidates to screen via the telephone. Do not wait too long (more than a week) to respond to an ad. If you do wait, the resume might not even be reviewed.

When applying for a position with a salary expectation above $50,000, wait at least a week before a resume is submitted. These highly-paid jobs take considerably more time and effort on the part of the recruiter to fill. Usually, there is a more in-depth review of preliminary qualifications. It may take several months to find the right candidate. In fact, results of a recent survey by Robert Half International indicate that it takes an average of three and one-half months to fill a top management job; two months for a middle management position; and one and one-half months for a staff position.

As a company starts to be more aggressive in their recruitment efforts, they often become more lenient in regards to the job's stated requirements. After screening several candidates, a company may change the profile of the person they seek. Time becomes an ally to the applicant. Should the resume be sent several weeks after the ad was run, you may be in a better position to receive a response from the company. If your salary goal is extremely high, consider sending in resumes approximately three to four weeks after the ad appears.

Salary expectations should determine the response timing to an advertisement. If the salary is less than $50,000, do it immediately. If more than $50,000, wait at least a week. The higher the salary, the longer you should delay

Remember, you must have an exceptional resume and cover letter that has been designed to grab the attention of the reader. A recruiter quickly screens through the unprofessionally prepared resumes and may skip over qualified candidates who do not know how to present themselves on paper. It happens in the real world! A resume should make an impression on the reader and pass the first screening. (See the Resume and Cover Letter Door for more details.)

Follow(n) Up Again? Make Sure You Do!

Play it again, Sam. Play it again.

–WOODY ALLEN
Circa 1936

As in any effective system, the loop must be closed in order for it to work properly. Likewise, it is essential in my PDQ job search system. Accurate records of job hunting activities allow for timely follow-up actions. If you do not have a personal computer to use, I recommend a 3 x 5" index card with the following format:

OPPORTUNITY FOLLOW-UP INFORMATION

COMPANY/POSITION: ____________________

ADDRESS: ____________________

CONTACT/PHONE: ____________________

SOURCE OF LEAD: ____________________

Newspaper Open Ad ____ Newspaper Blind Ad ____ Referral Letter ____

Employment Agency _____ Search Firm _____ Other ____________

DATE OF CONTACT/MAILING: ____________________

FOLLOW-UP DATE: ____________________

ACTION ITEMS: ____________________

____

RESULTS: ____________________

____

After the initial response to an open ad, you may receive either a call from the company with a request for additional information or a "Thanks, but no thanks." form letter.

If two weeks go by and there has not been any contact from the company, take the initiative and make a telephone call to the name of the person indicated in the ad, or the personnel department. The majority of applicants do not call, but wait to hear from them. Show the company your assertiveness with a follow-up telephone call and request an interview. This PDQ technique works surprisingly well, try it! The recruiter may be very apologetic for not responding sooner and is placed on the defensive. You therefore have an excellent opportunity to suggest an immediate interview.

Seeing Through ... Blind Ads

Amazing Grace, how sweet the sound, that saved a wretch like me.
I once was lost, but now am found. Was blind, but now I see.

– JOHN NEWTON

As previously mentioned, it is estimated that blind ads account for a high percentage of all published professional level positions. Blind ads are placed for many reasons. Two of the most common are:

1. Economic – Since the average cost of a business letter is between ten and fifteen dollars, the cost of responding mounts up quickly. A company does not want to bother responding to hundreds of resumes and letters.

2. Workforce Availability – A company may be planning a move into the area, a reorganization may be under consideration, or perhaps marginal performers are on the way out. With the placement of blind ads the company has the opportunity to judge the availability of replacement candidates. Search firms (see Door 5) also use blind ads extensively.

Carefully read the ads and look for any telltale clues that might identify the company. If you are astute, one of the advantages that can be derived from blind ads is the ability to zero in on a specific industry or company that is conducting a search. This provides a better opportunity to directly pursue the job, rather than just waiting for a response. For example, the following ad appeared in Sunday's paper.

ACCOUNTING MANAGER

A major semiconductor manufacturer located in the Southwest has an immediate need for an Accounting Manager. The successful candidate will have 8 to 10 years of general accounting experience in a manufacturing environment. You must possess the ability to take charge of a 10 person department and provide the necessary leadership to motivate and direct the staff.

We can provide you with an excellent opportunity for growth and development. Generous benefits, flexible working hours, along with a starting salary commensurate with your experience is offered. For immediate consideration send your resume and salary history to: The New Mexico Daily Globe, P.O.Box 1234, Albuquerque, New Mexico 95076

With a careful review of the wording, clues can be found to identify the company that placed the ad. Once the choices have been narrowed down to a few suspect companies, a campaign can be started to contact those firms and present qualifications. Let us carefully read the ad again, looking for clues:

1. We know the firm is a semiconductor company.
2. The company is located in the Southwest.
3. The firm has at least 10 people in the accounting department, so it cannot be a small company, probably somewhere in $100 million annual sales range.
4. The company offers flexible working hours.
5. It may be located around Albuquerque, since the ad was placed in the local paper.

You may ask yourself, "What do I do next?" Go to the library and research all the semiconductor manufacturers in the Southwest. The librarian can assist in locating the correct directories. Eliminate the smaller firms, since they normally would not have such a large accounting department. Then call the companies that remain and ask the public relations department some general questions about the company. Request information about the types of benefits that are offered employees. People in public relations always try to promote good aspects about their company. You might find that one of the companies offers flexible working hours as a benefit. Remember the clues?

Through the process of elimination, the search to identify the company that placed the ad is substantially narrowed. Now a more direct approach can be taken to make contact.

When two or three companies that could have placed the ad are identified, find the name of the Chief Financial Officer (CFO) of each suspect firm and send a personal introductory cover letter. Focus on specific career highlights that correlate with the requirements of the advertisement. If successful in identifying the correct company, a telephone call from the CFO may be forthcoming, or personnel directed to initiate contact. You might even find that one of the companies that did not have an opening is interested based on the unsolicited resume or cover letter received. Don't forget the PDQ follow-up approach previously outlined. Make a telephone call if there has been no response to letters.

If one puts in the necessary effort on this particular aspect of the PDQ job finding system, the odds of success are greatly increased. You will have navigated one more correct turn through the employment maze to a potential interview.

CAUTION

SWINGING DOOR!

A word of caution about blind ads. If an ad sounds exactly what you have been looking for and is very similar to current job responsibilities, guess what? It may be your present employer who placed the advertisement. I have seen this happen on too many occasions. When the company receives a resume from the incumbent, it becomes an embarrassment to all.

Out of ... "Position-Wanted" Ads

I don't like to lose, and that isn't so much because it is just a football game, but because defeat means the failure to reach your objective. I don't want a football player who doesn't take defeat to heart, who laughs it off with the thought, "Oh, well, there's another Saturday." The trouble in American life today, in business as well as in sports, is that too many people are afraid of competition. The result is that in some circles people have come to sneer at success if it costs hard work and training and sacrifice.

–KNUTE ROCKNE

Just look in the want ads section of the newspaper on any given Sunday and a few "Position Wanted" ads can be seen. These are brief advertisements placed by individuals seeking employment opportunities. People who place such ads hope a potential employer will read the paper in search of candidates with their specific skills. During my years in the personnel and human resources profession, I have never hired a person from a Position Wanted ad. The use of Position Wanted ads may lead you down a one way path to a dead end.

Personnel recruiters do not normally use the Position Wanted section as a recruitment source. Research indicates that only 3 to 4% of the people that place these ads are successful in landing a job through this method.

If still convinced that you can be successful utilizing this method, consider the cost involved. A small, one-column, three-inch ad costs about fifty to one hundred dollars, depending on the publication. If a display ad is used, three columns by three inches, the cost can run up to several hundred dollars. Check with the advertising department of the publication under consideration. They can provide all the details on how to submit ad copy.

I recommend placing a Position Wanted ad only if you are considered to be a technical employee in a specific occupation. For example, a bipolar design engineer with ten years of experience stands a much better chance of receiving a response than an entry-level, electronics technician. If you have a specialized talent that is in demand, you might consider placing a Position Wanted ad in a professional association newsletter. Don't pass up this excellent tool. Your colleagues probably read every issue, cover to cover.

The publishers of these periodicals have special rates and may place an ad for a discounted rate when a person is unemployed.

Be aware of the market conditions and demands for specific talents. Remember the basic economic theory of supply and demand. Not too many years ago when the aircraft industry was in a severe downturn, thousands of engineers were out of work. Some resorted to driving taxi cabs for a living. Today, those same engineers are in great demand. Since the market fluctuates throughout the year, it behooves one to stay abreast of what is happening in specific fields.

Check ... Lists and Directories

The doors of opportunity are marked "push" and "pull."

—ANON.

In the first part of this book I wrote about the possibility of relocation and its importance in the job hunting process. If geographical restrictions are imposed, the scope of the job search is dramatically reduced. On the other hand, if the search is opened nationwide, the source of published ads is not limited to just local newspapers.

In order to expand your campaign, one way to identify key personnel in various firms is to use directories. There are hundreds available with topics such as publishers, retailers, paper products, importers, glass manufacturers, food services, banks, electronics, drug companies, etc. Spend a day at your local library and first look for: The Guide to American Directories, B. Klein Publications, Coral Springs, Florida 33065. This publication describes 6000 companies in 250 subject categories. Research a specific industry directory where there is an interest in finding a job, e.g., electronics, food services, medical, etc. Find 30 to 40 companies and write down the name and address of key executives to contact later via direct mail.

Make sure the directories selected are current. Obsolete references serve no useful purpose and waste valuable time and effort.

In addition to directories, there is another route to find job openings. Several companies provide a list of open positions that appear in major newspapers and journals throughout the country. For the amount of information provided, it is relatively inexpensive, less than fifty dollars. Consider contacting the following sources:

1. Career Systems Inc. (306/689-3337) – company job requirements matched against submitted resumes.

2. CompuServe (800/595-2365) – computer data base of available jobs.

3. Career Links Inc. (800/331-7717) – jobs listed from ads across the country.

4. National Business Employment Weekly (212/808-6792) – consolidation of ads placed in all regional issues of the Wall Street Journal.

5. Federal Research Services Inc. (702/281-0200) – jobs available in the federal government.

A Double Take Cartoon

Amusement Parked ... or Job Fairs

Now this is the point. You fancy me mad. Madmen know nothing. But you should have seen me. You should have seen how wisely I proceeded—with what caution—with what foresight—with what dissimulation. I went to work!... I turned the latch of his door and opened it.... It took me an hour to place my whole head within the opening.... Upon the eighth night I was more than usually cautious in opening the door. A watch's minute hand moves more quickly than did mine. Never before that night had I felt the extent of my own powers—of my sagacity. I could scarcely contain my feelings of triumph. To think that there I was, opening the door, little by little ... and so I knew that he could not see the opening of the door, and I kept pushing it on steadily, steadily.

—EDGAR ALLEN POE
The Tell-Tale Heart

Another outside service that can prove very beneficial in finding your way through the employment maze is the use of "job fairs." These have emerged in the last few years as an excellent recruitment tool for companies and as an "on-line" job bank for individuals seeking new positions.

The way a job fair program works is very simple. Basically, the firms that exhibit pay a $2,000 to $3,000 fee for the opportunity to set up a booth in a hotel to recruit applicants. The booths and atmosphere are similar to trade shows.

"Manned" by personnel recruiters and technical professionals, most job fairs are geared towards those in a technical field who want to change jobs. Advertisements in local newspapers and trade publications that announce the time and place normally run a week or two prior to the opening date. Expect to see as many as 50 different companies, aggressively competing with each other for scarce technical talent.

Key Point If you are in a technical field, job fairs are an excellent means to land an interview. Introduce yourself to the recruiter and technical staff members at the booths and write down their names and telephone numbers for future use and reference. Discuss opportunities and have plenty of updated resumes available.

After the fair ends, write a letter to each of the representatives with whom you spoke. Emphasize interest in their company and the contribution you can make as a member of their staff. A call from the recruiter for an interview may be forthcoming.

CAUTION

SWINGING DOOR!

A word of caution. If you plan to attend one of these job fairs, make sure your present company does not have a representative there. Imagine the embarrassment when personnel people or even the boss observes an employee in discussion with the competition. You will be hard pressed to try and explain your presence at the fair and absence from the office.

Although these fairs are usually for technical personnel, there may also be openings for non-technical positions. Do not minimize efforts to talk with various representatives at the fairs just because the personnel staff is there to hire technical people. The recruiters may be aware of open positions in the firm that are non-technical. As the saying goes, "leave no stone unturned."

Revolving Doors ... A Review

Want ads only account for a small number of job opportunities available. However, one should not underestimate their power. Try to identify the various types of ads and then use them wisely. Also don't forget to use other lists, directories and job fairs. The key to your success is proper utilization of the process identified and following up until you make it through the maze.

DOOR 4

RESUMES & COVER LETTERS

S.O.S. (Send Out Signals)

'Tis the Season ... or
When Do Companies Hire?

Fact to the Future ... or Resumes

Weed 'em & Reap (the Benefits) ... or
Resume Data Sheets

ResuMAZE Architecture ... or
Styles of Resumes

Reservations About "Blankets" ... or
Cover Letters

DOOR 4

RESUMES & COVER LETTERS

S.O.S. (Send Out Signals)

The time to hesitate is through. No time to wallow in the mire....
Come on baby light my fire. Try to set the night on fire.

—THE DOORS
Light My Fire

The primary purpose of a resume is not to generate job opportunities, but instead is simply a means of presenting one's career history and qualifications. On the other hand, the cover letter is an excellent way of initiating contacts. Both have their place in the job search. As you move through this door, closely examine the development and timely usage of these tools. Each will play a key role during specific phases of the job search.

'Tis the Season ... or When Do Companies Hire?

This Gun's for Hire.... I never knew anybody who was unhappy with their job and was happy with their life. It's your sense of purpose. Now some people can find it elsewhere. Some people can work a job and find it someplace else...

–BRUCE SPRINGSTEEN, "THE BOSS"
From the book Glory Days by Dave Marsh, 1987

The selection of the proper time to start your job hunt campaign plays a significant role in the success or failure of your efforts through the employment maze. There are specific times during a calendar year that are better than others to begin the search.

Most companies run on the calendar year and start new budgets every January and as a result, there is an increase in want ads due to new personnel requisitions being approved. Employment hiring is strong until the start of summer, then it slows significantly due to vacations. Activity picks up again in September and continues until the middle of November. Finally, late in the year, companies cut expenses to make the year-end bottom line look good. New hiring is delayed, even if approvals have already been given. Keep these factors in mind in developing strategies. Incidentally, many people resist the urge to change jobs until after the new year because of vacations, potential bonuses, and other forms of compensation.

It does not matter what time of the year you send in an unsolicited resume. Companies really do not want them! The average personnel department receives thousands of unsolicited resumes each year and innumeral hours are needed just to handle this volume of paper. Those resumes are reviewed, logged into a resume data bank and/or filed, and then, a nice form letter is sent back to the applicant. Of course, there may be several resumes that match a specific need for a company, but the majority are just filed.

Fact to the Future ... or Resumes

"It's like Doc's always saying," Jennifer said to Marty.
"Yeah, I know," Marty replied. "If you put your mind to it, you can accomplish anything."
"That's good advice Marty."
"All right, OK, Jennifer. What, what if I send in the tape and they don't like it? I mean, what if they say I'm no good? What if they say, 'Get outta here kid, you've got no future?' I mean, I just don't think I can take that kind of rejection."

–BACK TO THE FUTURE

With a review of the PDQ techniques already discussed, you should be able to generate several ideas that lead down the correct path in a personalized job search. However, before the program can be put into action, be aware of the role the resume and cover letter play in the process.

Of the thousands of resumes received by companies each year, only a few make the grade. All others lack the necessary elements that set them apart as outstanding material. The development of a resume and several "focused" cover letters is of paramount importance to gain a competitive edge over the average job hunter.

There is no sense trying to make you a professional resume writer by reading a few pages in this or any other book. However, there are some fundamental concepts that need to be addressed in order to help you understand the maze of confusion on this topic. Answers to the following questions will be clarified:

1. What is a resume?

2. What is the resume supposed to accomplish?

3. What should a resume look like?

4. How should a resume be prepared?

The purpose of a resume or cover letter is to attract the reader's attention in a professional manner. Additionally, the material should answer some quick questions, e.g., "How can this person help solve my problems or help with our company's needs?" The value you can bring to the company should be evident in the resume or cover letter. This "value concept" of your worth to the organization cannot be over emphasized.

With vast piles of poorly prepared resumes being submitted by others, an outstanding resume needs to be developed. Your material is a direct reflection of you, consider it to be a billboard of yourself.

Proofread your resume and then have someone else proof it too. One small typo may put your resume in the trash. You'd be surprised how many I receive that have mistakes on them. If you have a computer, use a spelling checker!

If you are uncomfortable in trying to compose a resume, complete the resume data sheet discussed later in this section, then locate a professional resume writer. Look in the want ads or contact one of the larger national firms such as:

- Professional Resumes & Writing Service (800/824-5858)
- Resume Plus Inc. (212/661-2140)
- Effective Resumes (404/565-8890)

Depending on the services requested, the cost varies with the amount of background work needed, from as little as $50 to as much as $500. Discuss the type of format to be used and review a draft copy prior to printing the finished product. Keep in mind the resume is marketing you and better look like a million bucks!

Whether you choose to write your own resume or have a "professional" write one, you should know some of the basics. So let us examine some PDQ resume pointers.

PDQ RESUME POINTERS:

1. **Design the resume for a specific industry or company.** Use the same buzz words.

2. **Utilize positive, action verbs to describe accomplishments.** For example: directed, developed, implemented, organized, etc.

3. **Get down to the "nitty gritty" on what you have accomplished.** No need to be flowery. A generalized, verbose resume is a big turnoff. Focus on the "meat and potatoes" in terms of specific results instead of just listing your job functions. For example: reduced expenses 25% in one year, increased sales 20% over the previous year, increased production yield 18%.

4. **State your worth to the company.** By using this "value concept," the reader knows what contributions you can make that will impact their business. This PDQ technique not only asks for a job, it also shows why they need you!

5. **Reduce non-essential information.** If interest is created, other areas in your background will be addressed at the interview. Do not waste valuable "billboard space" with irrelevant information. I also discourage the use of any graphics, since they distract from the body of the material.

6. **Try to limit the size of the resume to two pages.** Obviously, your experience and salary will be the major factors that influence the length. Consider the audience. A recruiter becomes bored reading single-spaced, two or three page resumes all day long. The longest resume I have received was 27 pages. It was from a technical guru who listed every project he ever worked on. Unfortunately, the only points it scored was when I made a left-handed hook shot into the basket (waste). It was obvious that this person was disorganized in his thoughts and could not present himself clearly on paper. Remember, when writing a resume – quality words work, not quantity.

7. **Quality materials should be used when preparing the final product.** Never use plain white paper. I recommend a soft gray or ivory color. Use 20 or 24 lb. paper stock and never make copies. Always have the finished product printed with an offset press or a laser printer. The standard 8-1/2 x 11" size paper is the norm. Visit your local print shop. They can help with special printing needs.

8. **Do not list references, simply state that references are available upon request.** Although convenient for the recruiter, it can cause problems. You may quickly find that the trusted people listed on the resume are annoyed at all the calls. If an interviewer wants references immediately, request that they not be checked unless a job offer is forthcoming. The company can always make an offer contingent upon successful checks.

Three to five names should be available. Check with each person listed and obtain their approval before releasing the names. It is advisable to inform them to expect an inquiry from the company at which you interviewed. Give them information about the job that you applied for and the name of the person who will call. This provides adequate preparation time for your reference.

Since a good reference attests to your business experience and value, previous co-workers or bosses are recommended, not the views of your friends. You may want to have a close friend call to check the responses. Occasionally, someone may give out derogatory information. Correct your list when appropriate.

9. **Normally, you should not reveal current earnings unless requested in the advertisement.** Even then I would question the value of stating your salary. Over the years, my staff and I have placed hundreds of open and blind ads that requested salary information. On several occasions, my recruiters have received resumes as a result of an ad and eliminated the candidate because the stated salary was too high. Conversely, I have instructed staff members to call an applicant who looked good on paper, but had not revealed salary in the resume. An initial interview to screen the applicant was conducted over the telephone. If the recruiter was impressed, the potential employee was asked in for a personal interview. Although both applicants may have had the same salary, the candidate that did not reveal that information forced the company to initiate discussions, which uncovered a background that interested the company. Salary became a secondary issue for future negotiations. I suggest these simple guidelines be followed:

   - Provide the information when applying for a job with an anticipated salary of $25,000 a year or less and salary is requested.

   - Write down the anticipated salary requirements, not the current figure if the jobs salary is above $25,000 but less than $45,000.

   - With a salary range above $45,000, I recommend current salary never be revealed. Positions at that level and above are usually open for negotiation and a variety of compensation issues typically arise.

10. **Include personal data on a resume.** I recommend the following information be identified:

    - date of birth,
    - marital status,
    - number of children,
    - hobbies (optional).

    While this information has nothing to do with actual job requirements, the interviewer usually obtains these facts from questions anyway. If you do not include this data on the resume, volunteer it during the initial ice breaking stage of the interview. Do not waste time playing "24 questions". Convey the facts and move on to more serious questions.

    I have also seen resumes with the words, "Affirmative Action Candidate" printed or stamped on the front page. Don't do this. Sell yourself on qualifications. It is very unprofessional and will send out the wrong signals to a prospective employer.

Weed 'em & Reap (the Benefits) ... or Resume Data Sheets

Just the facts, Mamm. Just the facts.

—JOE FRIDAY
Dragnet, Tuesday, 1961

In order to effectively prepare a resume and cover letter, a review of previous work history is essential. The PDQ resume data sheet helps accomplish this task. Review the questions and write down as much information as possible. Later, edit unnecessary details for the final draft.

PDQ RESUME DATA SHEET

PERSONAL INFORMATION:

Name: ______________________________

Address: ______________________________

Phone (home): ______________________________

Phone (work): ______________________________

Date of Birth: ______________________________

Health: ______________________________

Marital Status: ______________________________

Children: ______________________________

EDUCATION:

School Attended	Year Graduated	Degree Obtained

List any awards or honors received.

____

____

____

List significant activities or achievements.

Did you pay for your education? What percentage? What percentage of time did you work while attending school?

SEMINARS/TRAINING: What seminars or training programs did you attend?

PROFESSIONAL ASSOCIATIONS/CIVIC GROUPS: List all professional associations and civic groups in which you are/were a member.

Do you hold professional designations? Have you held offices?

SPARE TIME ACTIVITIES: List the activities where you spend most of your free time, e.g., golf, tennis, racquetball, jogging, sailing, reading, writing, crafts, etc.

MILITARY SERVICE: List your military experience. What training did you receive? What was your highest rank attained? Did you receive any awards? Does any of your military experience relate to the job you seek?

____

____

WORK HISTORY: List current job and work backwards to your first. Use this format for each position.

Company: ______________________________________

Job Title: ______________________________________

Report To: ______________________________________

Industry: ______________________________________

Location: ______________________________________

Dates Worked: ___________________________________

Start Salary: ____________________________________

End Salary: _____________________________________

Reason Left: ____________________________________

____

____

RESPONSIBILITIES: Use this section to expand on your current and previous job duties and responsibilities. What was the job function? How many people were supervised? Where were you in the organizational hierarchy? What was your budget authority? Give as much detail as necessary.

____

____

____

ACHIEVEMENTS: What specific achievements were accomplished while in previous positions? Be very specific, list dollars, percentages, etc., referring to sales, expenses, profits, growth, yields, production rates and so forth. Remember, the added value that you identify and can offer a company enhances your job opportunities.

POLICY PROCEDURE DEVELOPMENT: Were you responsible for any major policy or procedure development in the company? What were they? What was the impact?

PATENTS & PUBLICATIONS: List all patents and publications.

ORGANIZATIONAL CHANGES: Were you involved in any organizational changes such as a merger or acquisition? What role did you play?

______

______

______

COMPENSATION HISTORY: Review your compensation history at this company. List percentages and frequency of increases. What perks did you have, i.e., company car, health club membership, lunch club membership, expense account, first class travel, etc. What promotions did you receive?

______

______

______

______

______

______

______

ResuMAZE Architecture ... or Styles of Resumes

The last thing that we discover in writing a book is to know what to put in the beginning.

–BLAISE PASCAL

In the volumes of information regarding the various types of resumes, there are three distinct formats used today.

1. Chronological/Historical – reverse time-based, current job first.
2. Functional/Department – organized by job function, e.g., sales.
3. Targeted/Achievement – results-oriented.

As Time Goes By ... Chronological/Historical Resumes

- Lists the most recent job first and moves backwards in time to the first position.
- An excellent format to use when there are no time breaks in service and you can show a successful career path of increasingly responsible positions.
- Not recommended if you want to change careers, have been a job hopper, or have been in the same job for an extended period of time. In these cases consider the functional format.

Vocations and Gaps ... Functional/Department Resumes

- Used when organizing abilities by vocational functions such as sales, marketing, manufacturing, personnel, or finance.
- Demonstrates expertise in specific functional areas.
- Most useful when changing fields, time gaps occur in employment, re-entering the job market after an absence, or when a number of different functional experiences are remotely related.

Bulls-eye ... Targeted/Achievement Resumes

- Focuses on specific characteristics and highlights outstanding accomplishments.
- Useful when you have identified a specific market to attack.
- Customized to highlight areas that would be of direct interest to the firm you are contacting. An example would be a bipolar integrated circuit design engineer targeting his/her resume to a semiconductor company that specializes in bipolar products.

Chronological / Historical Resume Example:

Thomas A. Wilson
3842 W. Danbury Road
Phoenix, Arizona 80532
(602)555-7965

OBJECTIVE: Human Resources Director for a pro-active multinational electronics organization.

WORK EXPERIENCE:

1984 to Present: Zxcor Electronics, Phoenix, Arizona

Personnel Manager: Managed a staff of four in a 700 employee company. Coordinated manpower planning programs in the domestic and offshore operations which resulted in 220 new hires in 10 months. Developed tax protection policies and processed all expatriate visa documents. Installed a job evaluation system including formal job descriptions, salary administration guidelines, and executive incentive programs. Revamped employee group health insurance programs, introducing cost containment provisions that resulted in a 15% premium reduction.

1980-1984: Convex Manufacturing Inc., Tucson, Arizona

Employment Supervisor: Responsible for the development and implementation of the annual manpower plan. With a staff of two recruiters hired an average of 20 employees per month over a two year period. Coordinated nationwide college recruitment activities with ten universities.

Chronological / Historical Resume Example (Continued):

Recruitment budget responsibility of $100,000. Developed and conducted in-house training of supervisory personnel in lawful interviewing practices.

1978-1980: Intermetic Electronics Inc., Tucson, Arizona

Recruiter: Responsible for the recruitment of all technical personnel. Placed advertisement within monthly budget allocation of $2,000.

Coordinated college recruitment of engineering graduates. Trained junior recruiters.

PROFESSIONAL ASSOCIATIONS: American Society of Personnel Administration

EDUCATION: B.S. Personnel Management, UCLA 1978

PERSONAL: Married, 2 children; Health - excellent

Will relocate

Functional /Department Resume Example:

DONALD R. WINSTON
1574 West Lake Drive
Bloomfield Park, New York 48345
(212)555-4356

OBJECTIVE: Senior Financial Administrative Officer

BACKGROUND SUMMARY: Experienced corporate officer with a 20 year track record in directing financial and administrative functions. Career span includes increasingly responsible positions from auditor in a "Big 8" CPA firm to Vice President Finance and Administration.

QUALIFICATIONS:

FINANCIAL ACHIEVEMENTS

* Responsible for evaluation and directing 20 acquisitions and mergers.

* Directed 5 public stock offerings, maintained coordination with the S.E.C. and other regulatory agencies.

* Established domestic and foreign banking relationships resulting in unsecured, guaranteed, 5 year, $25,000,000 line of credit at prime rate. Implemented cost containment program resulting in a $250,000 reduction of expenses in 6 months.

Functional/Department Resume Example (Continued):

* Developed corporate credit policy reducing bad debt write offs from 32% to 7%.

* Initiated the reduction and consolidation of corporate insurance coverages. Reduced the number of carriers from 10 to 2 with annualized savings of $475,000 in premiums.

ADMINISTRATIVE ACCOMPLISHMENTS

* Designed a computerized "MRP" system for corporate purchasing, reduced lead times, and eliminated duplicated functions.

* Planned and implemented the total installation of worldwide telecommunications equipment, including on-line daily factory production results.

WORK HISTORY:

1983 - Present	World Products Inc., V.P. Finance/Administration
1980 - 1983:	Zetec Corporation, Comptroller
1975 - 1980:	ADP Ultrasonics Inc., Accounting Manager
1970 - 1975:	Barrons Manufacturing Inc., Credit Manager
1965 - 1970:	Smith, Jones, and Mitchell., Auditor

EDUCATION:

MBA: University of California 1965
B.S.: Accounting, University of California 1963

PROFESSIONAL STANDINGS: CPA designation 1969

Targeted/Achievement Resume Example :

Peter Anderson
27 Wayford Avenue
Austin, Texas 78781

OBJECTIVE: MOS Design Manager

ACHIEVEMENTS:

* Supervised a team of 25 engineers designing 4Kb and 16Kb SRAMS, 8Kb, 16Kb, 32Kb and 64Kb EPROMS and 64K ROMS.

* Project engineer designing second and third generation triple poly 64Kb and 256Kb DRAMS.

* Designed a P-Channel silicon gate ROM and an N-channel metal gate with on-chip drivers.

* Developed a linear/digital CMOS version of a bipolar sensor chip.

* Coordinated efforts of 6 engineers in the design of various advanced high-speed gate arrays and standard cell arrays utilizing 1.0 micron design rules.

* Developed software to extract and characterize transistor SPICE modeling parameters.

* 5 Integrated Circuit Patents issued.

Targeted/Achievement Resume Example (Continued):

WORK HISTORY:

1982-Present:	Dart Semiconductor, MOS Section Supervisor
1979-1982:	Ztec Semiconductor, MOS Design Engineer
1975-1979:	Holetech Inc., Device Modeling Engineer

EDUCATION:

M.S.E.E.	University of Southern California, 1975
B.S.E.E.	University of Utah, 1973

PERSONAL: Married, 1 child; Health, excellent

Reservations About "Blankets" ... or Cover Letters

I am tired of talk that comes to nothing. It makes my heart sick when I remember all the good words and all the broken promises. There has been too much talking by men who had no right to talk. Too many misinterpretations have been made; too many misunderstandings have come up....

–CHIEF JOSEPH
Nez Perce Tribe

The function of the cover letter is to create an awareness that you have qualities the hiring company needs. The utilization of proper cover letters in a direct mail campaign is one of the most successful methods used to generate interviews. Follow these PDQ cover letter pointers:

1. Address the letters to a specific individual, usually the manager of the department where you are attempting to gain entrance.

2. Keep the length to one page. Use personal stationery of a soft gray or ivory color. Always match the color to that of the resume.

3. Start with a comment about their company, e.g., "I recently read in the Wall Street Journal that your firm is expanding operations in the West."

4. Focus on the "value concept." Stress your achievements so it becomes obvious to the reader the benefits that you can bring to their company.

5. If you have experience in a specific industrial segment, emphasize continued interest in remaining in that industry.

6. Do not ask for a job in the letter. Instead ask for a meeting to share some unique ideas that would be beneficial to their organization.

7. State that you will call in a few days to set up a meeting.

On the following pages are examples of cover letters that may be used when dealing with various contacts. Note how with slight changes, you can send letters to "cold" contacts, open and blind advertisements, and search firms.

Sample Cover Letter for Unsolicited or "Cold" Contact:

Dear _______________:

Your company's intention to expand factory operations to the Dallas area from Chicago was outlined in the Dallas Globe last week. The article was informative and described your firm's continued growth through a commitment to excellence.

Being a successful professional in the personnel field with 12 years experience, I have been involved with plant start-up operations. I believe my expertise in this area will be of interest to you.
As Personnel Manager with a major manufacturer, I was fully responsible in the establishment of the personnel function when our company relocated to Dallas from Detroit.

MAJOR ACHIEVEMENTS INCLUDE:

* Initially hired five personnel staff members.

* Developed census plan with plant manager that resulted in 500 new hires within 10 months.

* Implemented a corporate communications program, increasing employee morale.

* Instituted health insurance cost containment program, resulting in first year claims reduction of $75,000.

* Actively participated in civic organizations and established new relationships between the company and the community.

I am 32 years old, married with 2 children. I received my B.S. in Personnel Management from Ohio State University in 1975.

The opportunity to discuss some of my ideas that will make the relocation of your operation a complete success would be mutually beneficial. I will call you in a few days to arrange a meeting.

Sincerely,

Christina Merideth

Sample Cover Letter for an Open Advertisement:

Dear_______________:

I read with great interest your advertisement requesting highly motivated sales professionals to submit their qualifications for your position of Area Sales Manager. My background matches the requirements that you seek.

The last 15 years in direct sales and management enabled me to gain invaluable expertise in my profession. Briefly, I would like to summarize my qualifications.

As Regional Sales Manager, I coordinated the activities of three district managers and 12 sales representatives, where sales increased three consecutive years (8%, 12%, and 21%) above budget. The current annual sales run rate is $18 million.

I reduced the regional sales to expense ratio from 22% to 13% in eight months and negotiated contracts for two new regional distributors resulting in first year point of sales of $2.5 million. Also, I designed and implemented an automatic quotation follow-up program, which provided vital feedback to product managers. This resulted in competitive pricing structures.

At age 41, I am married with 4 children and in excellent health. I graduated from Stanford in 1972 with a B.S. in Marketing, and in 1983 received an MBA from UCLA.

I have outgrown the opportunities available at my current firm and seek a new association with a growth company such as yours.

Enclosed is my resume for your review. I would appreciate the opportunity to speak with you personally to further elaborate on the value I can bring to your company. I look forward to a mutually beneficial discussion.

Sincerely,

Christina Merideth

Sample Cover Letter to Search Firms:

Dear_______________:

In the course of one of your client's searches, you may have a need for a seasoned sales professional. The last 15 years in direct sales and management enabled me to gain invaluable expertise in my profession. Briefly, I would like to outline several significant achievements in my career:

As Regional Sales Manager, I coordinated the activities of three district managers and 12 sales representatives, where sales increased three consecutive years (8%, 12%, and 21%) above budget. The current annual sales run rate is $18 million.

I reduced the regional sales to expense ratio from 22% to 13% in eight months and negotiated contracts for two new regional distributors resulting in first year point of sales of $2.5 million. Also, I designed and implemented an automatic quotation follow-up program, which provided vital feedback to product managers. This resulted in competitive pricing structures.

At age 41, I am married with 4 children and in excellent health. I graduated from Stanford in 1972 with a B.S. in Marketing, and in 1983 received an MBA from UCLA.

I have outgrown the opportunities available at my current firm and seek a new association with a growth company. My compensation requirements exceed $75,000. Enclosed is my resume for your review.

In the event my qualifications meet the needs of one of your clients, I would appreciate the opportunity to speak with you personally to further elaborate on the value I can offer. I will call your office in a few days.

Sincerely,

Christina Merideth

Notice in the cover letter to the search firm that I stated compensation requirements exceed $75,000. This practice is acceptable since it does not reveal current salary. The search firm then has a good idea where the candidate fits in relation to specific requirements of a particular search.

Revolving Doors ... A Review

The importance of outstanding resumes and cover letters cannot be overemphasized. These documents make the first impression (or perhaps the last) and are the keys to open the door to a potential interview. Remember, the entire purpose of a cover letter is to generate interest. The resume should present your career history and qualifications. Without the right combination, you will never get to the interview or your foot in the door.

Most of my professional associates in the Human Resources field look for specific information on a cover letter or resume that enables them to make quick decisions whether or not to pursue an individual. Your job in presenting materials is to create interest. If you succeed, a telephone call should follow. The achievement of a major milestone, obtaining an interview, will have been accomplished. Utilize every tool available to gain a competitive advantage over the average job hunter.

Yes, my husband is a workaholic too. Everytime I mention work, he needs a drink!

A Double Take Cartoon

DOOR 5

OUTSIDE HELP

Grouping in the Dark

A Key Combination ... or Employment Agencies

"Seek and Ye Shall Find" ... or Search Firms

It's Not a Dead End ... or Outplacement Firms

DOOR 5

OUTSIDE HELP
Grouping in the Dark

A mother had been lecturing her small son, stressing that we are in this world to help others. He considered this for some time, then asked somberly: "What are the others here for?"

—ANON.

In the preceding door, the resume and cover letter were identified as vital tools in the process of obtaining an interview. As you enter this door, the use of employment agencies, search firms, and outplacement companies will be highlighted. Pay special attention to the methodology of dealing with these firms, for unless you know the secret keys, energy and time will be needlessly wasted.

A Key Combination ... or Employment Agencies

The greatest thoughts seem degraded in their passage through little minds. Even the winds of heaven make but mean music when whistling through a keyhole.

—ANON.

An employment agency is a firm that works either independently or directly for a client company to fill a job vacancy. Paid on a contingency basis, AFTER the job is filled, they do not usually have an exclusive for the opening in the client company. Positions available are usually less than $50,000 a year in salary. Find the yellow pages telephone book and locate "employment agencies" or "placement firms." In a major city dozens of firms are listed. Why are there so many in this line of business? The employment agency business is very opportunistic and can lead to tremendous financial rewards in a short period of time.

There are two kinds of employment agencies: 1) the agencies that work and require payment from you, and 2) agencies that work for a company who has an open position and are paid by that company. Whoever the agency works for, pays the fee.

I have been asked innumerable times whether or not one should pay an up-front fee to an employment agency. Unfortunately, the answer is not clear. It depends on the uniqueness of the situation. If you are just starting out in your career and have little or no work experience, you may have to pay a fee. Agencies that require payment by the applicant usually have a specific job available that you can apply for immediately. Normally, these openings have a starting annual salary of $12,000 to $20,000.

If you find an agency that requires an up-front fee, proceed cautiously. Check with the Better Business Bureau about the credibility of the agency. Review their materials and see if they are a member of any professional employment agency association. Ask about their success in placing applicants and how long they have been in business. Never jump into any contractual arrangements based on the emotional hype of the representative. Sit on your decision for a day or two. Evaluate other alternatives before making a final commitment to pay a fee.

Should you decide to pay the fee, make sure there are complete details of the services provided. Clarify any misunderstandings or unusual wording in the contract. Follow up weekly with the representative. Be tactful, but push for activity, i.e., job interviews. One final note, any money that you pay in relationship to a new job search is tax deductible. Keep accurate records of any financial outlays during the search activity and bring them to the attention of your tax consultant.

Since most job seekers are already familiar with employment agencies that they have to pay, I will concentrate the rest of my discussion on those that are paid by the hiring firm. This type of agency solicits job orders from companies, not the other way around. A company with a job opening may allow an agency to submit resumes for review, but are in no way obligated to pay any up-front fees. Agencies recruit at the same time as the company's own personnel people. When a position is difficult to fill and an agency has the right candidate at the right time, the company may review the resume and possibly interview the candidate and if the applicant meets all the qualifications of the position, an offer may be made. There is another point to consider. They have no obligation to hire you and may continue to search until a suitable candidate is found.

Cost is a major consideration when a company considers the use of an employment agency. The rates vary depending on competition, but the rule of thumb is 20 to 30% of the annual base salary offered. When a company looks for a candidate to fill a $40,000 per year job, it could cost a fee of $8,000 to $12,000. Keep in mind that an agency directs their efforts to the place that has the best chance of generating the next meal ticket.

Remember, all companies do not utilize employment agencies to assist in filling jobs. If you depend solely on an agency, it can substantially limit your exposure to openings. Don't put all your eggs in one basket. The use of an employment agency is just one more tool to be used in a job search campaign. Company-paid employment agencies can be categorized into two major types:

- Industry agencies
- Occupation agencies

Agencies that specialize in a specific industry segment usually have been in business the longest. For example, such a firm may have selected to work only in the banking industry. The other type of agency works with specific occupations. They recruit people with skills that can be used in any industry. Specializations may include data processing, accounting, personnel, or facilities engineering. Individuals possessing varied skills can work in many industries as compared to the bank manager, who is best suited for the banking industry.

Sorry guys, I know you all have banking experience, but ...

A Double Take Cartoon

If you are in the job market with a salary expectation of under $50,000, employment agencies may be able to assist. Remember the network set up earlier? Check with your Networkers and ask for a referral to a reputable employment agency. The chances are that the names of several local, as well as out-of-state firms, can be obtained. Research these companies with the Better Business Bureau for any complaints issued against them. Select a minimum of three to a maximum of five to approach. Make sure to distinguish between the two types previously discussed, (industry and occupation) and select the appropriate firms that fit your situation.

Contact these organizations with a cover letter that outlines your qualifications. After allowing sufficient time for the letter to arrive, call the agency and ask to speak with a representative in regards to the initial correspondence. Several questions will be asked that pertain to your current job, career goals, availability for relocation, and salary. Be prepared to discuss this information in depth. The representative will complete a data sheet from the information provided. If the firm is out of town, they will require that an updated resume be sent. If a computer system is used, information is entered into a data base, which allows the agency to match your qualifications with a current job search assignment.

Arrange a visit to the agency. Make an appointment to see your potential representative. Do not hesitate to ask questions. How long have they been in business? How large is the organization? What is their sales volume? What are the qualifications of the representative? Can they provide references? At the completion of the meeting, assess the discussion. Make a decision to work with them or pursue another company that meets your needs.

Key Point

Be aware of a critical point when dealing with agencies. These firms try to convince you that they are the only company that should be utilized. Remember, there is no law that says a person must work with only one employment agency at the same time. However, I would not broadcast this to the agencies involved.

There may not be any word from an agency for weeks or even months after the initial contact. They spend most of their time on the candidates that give them the best return on their investment. If there is not an opening that meets your profile, little goes into the marketing effort. This is why I recommend the use of more than one agency. Follow up four to six weeks after the initial contact. Don't be surprised if the first recruiter you dealt with is not with the firm. Employment agencies have a very high turnover rate due to the competitive nature of the business. When contact is made, express continued interest to the representative and inquire about the efforts made in your behalf. Ask what steps have been taken and what is planned next. Remember that old saying, "the squeaky wheel gets the grease."

CAUTION

SWINGING DOOR!

Tell the agency not to present credentials and qualifications to any company without prior discussion and your approval. Some firms use a "shotgun approach" to market a candidate. They may want to do a mass mailing of resumes to dozens of companies with the hope of drawing attention. It is a simple number's game. The more resumes sent out, the better the odds that one may hit. Protect yourself against this type of activity. Too many unnecessary eyes see resumes and word could get back to a current employer. The only exception to this rule is if you are unemployed.

Employment agencies serve a useful purpose in the business world. When the decision is made to utilize their services, a thorough analysis of the firm selected is of prime importance. Careful scrutiny of the agency's efforts can prevent wrong turns in the employment maze and increase the chances of a successful search.

"Seek and Ye Shall Find" ... or Search Firms

What we see depends mainly on what we look for.

—JOHN LUBBOCK

A search firm is an organization that has been hired by a client company to find a qualified candidate for a specific opening. Although they have the same purpose as an employment agency, i.e., to connect job applicants with opportunities, this is where the similarity stops. The search firm is contracted by a company on a retainer basis, usually with a part of their fee paid up-front. These firms can receive a fee up to 35% of the annual salary of the candidate, plus all related expenses, e.g., travel or telephone. With this type of cost involved, one can see why companies are very cautious in placing assignments with search firms.

Large companies usually retain search firms to fill critical positions. Occasionally, a small or start-up company utilizes their services. Companies use search firms for the major positions that require a specific set of skills and experiences. They understand the need for such services in order to fill upper-level positions. The company pays a search firm to seek out the best available candidate that exists, even if that person is not in the market for a job. Firms with openings realize that the best candidates are normally employed and satisfied in their present situation. These individuals would therefore not necessarily be looking to change jobs. The task of the search firm is to find and convince key people that the employment opportunity offers many advantages over their current position.

Only a seasoned professional in the search business is able to produce the results expected by their clients on a consistent basis. The recruiters understand the value of developing long-term relationships with clients and usually have more tenure than their counterparts who work in employment agencies. These search recruiters are more systematic in their approach to an assignment and do not take on the representation of just any person who sends in a resume. Contacting several of these firms is essential to cover the vast availability of jobs nationwide.

The executive search firm utilizes many different methods to help identify candidates for current and future searches. Search firms may employ junior recruiters or sourcing personnel who review professional journals, newspapers, press releases, company telephone books, organizational charts, or personal contacts within an organization. These sources supply the recruiters with information about up and coming people in business and industry. A file is usually started on an individual who has demonstrated a fast track record. Various clippings of articles and other items of interest are retained for future reference. As new assignments are awarded, search firms access their data banks and try to match the candidates qualifications on file to the requirements of the client.

Try to get your name into print. Write an article and submit it for publication or become a spokesperson at a major convention or conference. It looks great on your resume and may draw the attention of a search firm.

One of the more successful methods used by search firms is direct mail. As a Human Resources professional, I have received letters from search firms that read something like the example on the following page.

Search Letter Example

Dear Mr.Dombroski:

As a leading executive placement firm, we have been requested by one of our major clients to conduct a search for a seasoned human resources executive.

Our client's headquarters is located in a medium size city in the Midwest. Sales currently exceed $100 million with 20% growth expected this year.

We are currently evaluating candidates to fill a vacancy for Vice President Human Resources due to a recent promotion. The successful candidate should have at least 15 years experience in increasingly responsible positions.

Through your professional associations with various colleagues, you may be aware of an individual, perhaps yourself, who could have an interest in this outstanding opportunity. I would appreciate your cooperation in referring my name to that person. I can be contacted at 602/555-1212. Rest assured, confidentiality will be maintained. Your professional assistance is greatly appreciated.

Sincerely yours,

Jonathon Deer

While there are many variations to this type of letter, you can see what the search firm is trying to accomplish. First, the recruiter is briefly outlining an excellent opportunity (whetting the reader's appetite). Second, the recruiter is being very tactful in requesting a referral or a direct response from the reader.

If you receive one of these letters and the position is of interest, contact the search firm. They would not send a letter to an unqualified candidate. Be alert for these types of opportunities, they are an excellent means of unlocking the door to secure an interview.

Occasionally, a search firm runs a blind advertisement to test the waters as to how many qualified people are available for a specific assignment. Keep in mind a previous comment. As many as 300 responses may be received from a blind ad. The search firm then has a reasonable source of candidates without having to identify themselves.

A search firm may also place open ads in publications such as the Wall Street Journal. Here, they identify themselves as being retained by a major client to conduct a search. Many executives respond to advertisements based on the firm's reputation. If you observe one of these ads, but it does not match the specific type of position that is of interest, write down the name of the firm and individual listed in the ad. Send out an introduction letter directed to the individual.

Being in the right place at the right time holds true with search firms. The sooner contact is made with them, the better. Search firms have retainer contracts with major companies to fill professional positions at all levels. They may have a current search assignment that matches your specific qualifications.

If you meet the salary criteria guideline ($50,000 a year or more), I recommend selection of two or three search firms. Find out the names of their recruiters. Ask people in your network if they are familiar with the particular search firm under consideration. Call the firm and ask to speak to one of the search consultants. You may be screened out, but it is worth the effort. Again, try my PDQ "After Five" approach – when most clerical employees are gone and the search consultant typically answers the telephone. Recruiters work many late hours calling candidates at home.

When a cover letter is used to make the initial contact, again be sure to address it to a specific individual within the search firm. Invest a few dollars for a rubber stamp that states, "Confidential to be opened by addressee only" and stamp the envelope. In most cases the letter is not opened by a screening clerical person. The correspondence should briefly outline your decision to seek a new career opportunity. Summarize major accomplishments and be specific about achievements. Make sure to include career goals and timetables. Reveal compensation expectations, not actual salary. Provide a telephone number where you can be reached during the day, not just a home telephone number. Make it as easy as possible for the recruiter to make contact.

After waiting three or four weeks and an acknowledgement of the letter has not been received, take a more aggressive approach to contact recruiters. One of my PDQ methods that works is to send a mailgram. In the mailgram, refer to the first letter and provide enough information about yourself that jogs the memory of the recruiter. The first letter or resume may have already been placed in a computer data base file, but is just sitting there collecting micro dust. Several days later, call the office and ask to speak with the person to whom the mailgram was sent.

Key Point To make a lasting impression, send a letter via mailgram. Just call your local Western Union operator and dictate the letter. The cost is inexpensive, about $10 to $20 for fifty words, and arrives the next business day. Mailgrams are normally opened by the person to whom addressed and are not screened out by a secretary.

Once contact is made, it is important to sell yourself over the telephone. Be prepared to answer many questions similar to those presented in the following chapter on interviews. If the search firm is local, push to schedule an interview with the recruiter. Assertiveness is an admirable quality. A face-to-face relationship goes farther than one over the telephone or by mail. For a small fee (around $10), the following firms can provide lists of current professional and executive search firms.

1. Dunn's National Directories of Professional and Executive Recruiters (800/845-2307)

2. The Recruiting and Search Report (904/235-3733)

3. Custom Databanks (212/888-1650). If you have a personal computer, you can purchase a $75 diskette that contains the names and addresses of over 700 headhunters, who provide search firm services. It can sort by city, state, specific industry, high salaries ($50,000+), or retained firms.

The establishment of a mutually beneficial relationship is of paramount importance in dealing with an executive search firm and one should make every effort possible to develop it. Remember, the search firm is trying to match specific individual skills and traits to the requirements of their client. If you can demonstrate to the search consultant that you have what their client wants, the next door that opens may be to that all important interview.

It's Not a Dead End ... or Outplacement Firms

Just think how happy you'd be if you lost everything you have right now – then get it back again.

–LEONARD M. LEONARD
Journal of Living

Many companies face the unenviable task of terminating employees. When executive-level employees are involved, they feel an obligation to provide some type of assistance. Companies do not want to just put an employee "on the street." Out of such concerns came the birth of outplacement firms. Companies started soliciting assistance from third party organizations to give terminated employees professional help in preparation for a new job search. These firms emerged in the early 70's and have grown steadily into a major business segment of the '80's and '90's.

Through the use of outplacement firms, companies feel they provide a service for the terminated employee. The company's conscience is "clear" by offering the employee professional, outside assistance in finding a new position. While the service is expensive, 10 to 20% of the salary of the terminated employee, the company rationalizes the expense. Likewise, the employee is usually very appreciative of this type of assistance paid for by their former employer.

If you are ever asked to resign, try to convince the company to pay the cost of an outplacement firm. The use of this service shortens the process of finding a new position.

One of the major benefits of an outplacement firm is the help in the psychological letdown that is experienced. Losing a job ranks near the top of the list of major events that severely impacts our lives. Unless you are

"Superman," professional assistance is needed to get through the rough times. Reality sets in very quickly when you are still looking for a position and all the severance pay is gone. Naturally, if fortunate enough to secure another position in a short period of time, there is less trauma.

If your employer agrees to pay for the use of an outplacement firm, the following is an example of what can be expected:

1. Time may be spent with a psychologist, depending on the sophistication of the outplacement firm. One of the objectives is to help a person through the transition from employment to unemployment. Additionally, you may be asked to take a number of tests that identify personality characteristics. The results are compiled and recommendations are made on how to best approach the job search.

2. The next step in the process is meeting with the outplacement team. They provide counseling throughout the entire association with their firm. An in-depth review of background and experience is made and a preliminary marketing strategy developed.

3. After much discussion and evaluation, a formalized marketing approach is specifically designed and presented for your review. This includes the preparation of written materials such as resumes, cover letters, and introduction letters.

4. Many firms conduct a mock interview and video tape the session. The team then critiques and provides direction on how to improve your interviewing skills.

5. A final review of the customized marketing plan and written materials is made. After everyone is satisfied, the actual plan is then put into effect.

While this is a simplified version of the actual process, it shows how these firms can be very useful in job hunting. In fact, some outplacement firms I have spoken with boast a very high success rate. That is, 85 to 90% of their clients find and accept a new job within 6 months or less.

If you are not fortunate enough to have the employer pay the cost of an outplacement firm, help can still be obtained. For a reduced rate, many outplacement firms provide a modified version of the full service normally offered. With these reduced services, one can expect good verbal counseling, but limited assistance in the actual preparation of written materials, e.g., resumes and cover letters. A list of materials is usually offered that can be researched on various topics such as writing resumes and cover letters, networking, and interview techniques. They might even suggest that you read this book! A 10% fee of your previous annual salary should be expected. Utilizing the entire service can cost as much as 20% of previous salary depending on your job level and services requested.

CAUTION

SWINGING DOOR!

Be sure to review the terms and conditions of the contract before signing to use outplacement programs. A misunderstanding halfway through the process of what services you thought were to be provided can be very costly in time and money.

Outplacement firms are here to stay. In addition to the one-person consultant firms that perform outplacement activities, there are approximately 150 major outplacement companies with branch locations throughout the country. After the stock market crash in 1987, one firm received requests to assist over 20,000 unemployed professionals. Consider all the facts very carefully prior to spending any money. Caveat emptor – let the buyer beware.

Revolving Doors ... A Review

So far, I have reviewed several topics in my PDQ job search system on ways to get an interview. This door concentrated on obtaining outside help. Employment agencies, search firms, and outplacement firms all have their doors open, but it is up to you when to choose to open one.The next vital step is the actual face-to-face confrontation. In the following chapter, the preparation phase and actual implementation of guidelines used during an interview are detailed.

DOOR 6

THE INTERVIEW

The “Route” of the Problem

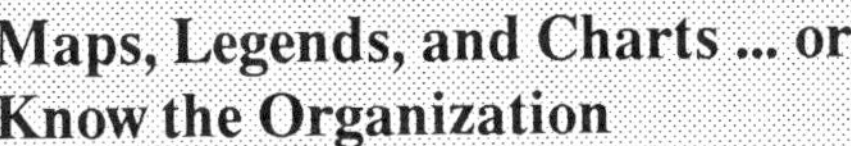

Maps, Legends, and Charts ... or
Know the Organization

Curves Ahead ... or Body Language

U-Turn to At"tire" ... or How to Dress

Right & Wrong Turns ... or
Interview Do’s & Don’ts

You Are What You Meet ... or The Arrival

Gearing Up ... or Survival Questions

Once More with Feeling ... or Follow up

DOOR 6

THE INTERVIEW
The "Route" of the Problem

Muad'Dib could indeed, see the future, but ... could not always choose to look across the mysterious terrain. He tells us that a single obscure decision of prophecy, perhaps the choice of one word over another, could change the entire aspect of the future. He tells us, "The vision of time is broad, but when you pass through it, time becomes a narrow door." And always, he fought the temptation to choose a clear, safe course, warning – "That path leads ever down into stagnation."

– FRANK HERBERT
Dune

All material covered thus far has been a prelude to one of the most exciting parts of a job search, the interview. Being on the other side of the employment desk for over 20 years, I can say without hesitation that the interview is the most critical phase of the hiring process. After dozens of hours spent to secure and prepare for the interview, everything hinges on the 30 to 60 minutes available to sell yourself. This door presents the basics about the interview process and how to maximize your efforts. Knowledge of the following is essential if one is to be successful when faced with an interview: knowing the organization; body language; dressing for success; and interviewing techniques. Without total comprehension of this information, you may wander aimlessly in the employment maze for years.

Maps, Legends, and Charts ... or Know the Organization

To be able to answer a question clearly is two-thirds of the way to getting it answered.

—ANON.

Prior to any interview, it is imperative that you learn as much as possible about the company. Research everything available on the firm. Obtain copies of annual reports, Dunn & Bradstreet analysis, marketing brochures, newspaper and magazine articles, press releases, etc. Find out what products they make and their markets. Check out the key players, the management that runs the company. Go to the library and look up "Who's Who" in the industry. Use directories as a source of information. The librarian has a wealth of knowledge and can assist in finding the necessary data. Just ask for it!

After you have sufficiently researched the company, formulate a number of key questions to ask the interviewer. Information you need to know should include:

- Why does the opening exist?
- What happened to the last person in the job?
- What is management's guiding philosophy of operation? Are they people orientated? Are they opportunistic? Do they believe in strong customer support? Do they concentrate strictly on the bottom line?
- In what direction is the company moving?
- What is the corporate culture? Ask the interviewer for an opinion.
- What are some of the most difficult problems that the company is facing today?
- How is the overall morale in the company?

- Is the company going through a merger or acquisition? If so, what is the impact on the position?
- Has there been any major managerial changes in the last six months?
- Is the company profitable?
- What about company sales? Growth rate?

From research conducted on the company, you should be able to answer a number of these questions. However, it is important to note the perceptions of the interviewer when answering questions. A clue to potential problem areas in the company, or verification of strong points may be gained. Based on the answers received during the interview, begin to formulate an opinion whether the company is a place in which you would like to work.

Being knowledgeable about their business demonstrates that there is genuine interest on your part. I am always impressed when an applicant begins to ask detailed questions about my company. In some cases the applicants know more about company events than our employees. Always remember, knowledge is the key that will unlock the door to success.

Curves Ahead ... or Body Language

On the road again.
Going places that I've never been.
Seeing things that I may never see again.
On the road again.

—WILLIE NELSON

During your career, I am sure that you have heard or read about "body language." Eye movements, facial expressions, hand and leg movements, and posture convey a great deal about attitudes in various situations. Don't underestimate the value of learning to read the language of the body.

Body movement communicates non-verbal signals. An understanding of these signs adds to the ability to effectively control the interview. Remember, you need to be aware of your own "language," as well as the interviewer's. Some of the more common signals and their meanings are:

- Folded Arms — a very defensive position. The person may be thinking, "prove it to me."
- Crossed Legs — somewhat bored, may be defensive.
- Tilted Head — interested in what the other is saying.
- Stroking the Chin — still thinking about the subject and has not made up their mind.
- Fingers in a "Church Steeple" Position — very positive, confident.
- Tightly Clenched Hands — uptight, not relaxed, could be getting hostile.
- Clearing Throat — uncertain or apprehensive.
- Touching the Nose — may doubt or not understand the statements.

If familiar with reading body language, you will know what signals the interviewer is sending and be able to adjust your presentation. Many books have been written on this subject and I strongly suggest to go to the local book store and purchase a copy, e.g., How To Read A Person Like A Book by Gerald Nierenberg and Henry Calero. This book is in paperback form and the cost is minimal. It would be a good addition to your library.

There is another part of the body that has been getting lots of "looks," i.e., the eyes. According to Dr. Allen Konopacki, a noted behavioral scientist and President of Incomm International Inc., "Eye language is more accurate than body language when it comes to understanding how people are responding to information." He further states in the April, 1987 Successful Meeting Magazine, "Eye movements are often involuntary and are, therefore, much more apt to reflect an individual's thought process." For example, eyes focused straight ahead may indicate daydreaming or being uninvolved. If the other person is too focused, you may be "tuned" out. When interviewing, do not stare, instead, glance at the person every few seconds to see how they are responding. If that person's eyes are looking upward to your right, they are logically analyzing your comments. Eyes looking upward to your left indicate an even more intense concentration on your statements. Eyes that look away from you may indicate a lack of further interest.

As a very familiar saying goes, "You can't judge a book by its cover." However, a significant first impression, either good or bad, will be made. The way a person physically looks creates a picture in the mind of the interviewer and is a significant factor in whether the hiring process continues or terminates. The way people dress has a direct bearing on the end results. Let us now examine how to properly dress to make that first, good impression.

U-Turn to At"tire" ... or How to Dress

Say Hey! ... Lookin' good!

—WILLIE "MAZE"
San Francisco, Circa 1959

Have you wondered why manufacturers spend millions each year on new packaging designs for their products? It's very simple, they want to make a good visual impression on the shopper, resulting in higher sales of their product. The way one dresses makes a strong visual impression. Everything a person wears sends out messages that can be interpreted as either positive or negative.

According to John Molloy, America's first "wardrobe engineer" and author of Dress for Success and The Woman's Dress for Success Book, "The way we dress has remarkable impact on the people we meet professionally or socially and greatly (sometimes crucially) affects how they treat us." He also states that both men and women have the tendency to dress for failure.

The critical task is to dress for the position that you seek, not for the one you already have. It becomes of paramount importance to learn the acceptable dress for the particular situation.

While I cannot examine every detail of dress in this section, here are several PDQ Dress Points.

PDQ DRESS POINTS:

1. Observe the dress of the people in the company where the interview is to be held.

2. Men should always wear a suit, preferably blue, grey, or beige. Shirts should be white or blue and worn with a solid color tie. Shoes should be the traditional wingtip or plain lace-up variety. Black or brown colors are the most acceptable.

3. The preferred type of dress for a woman is a skirted suit. Coordinated color outfits are a dark grey suit with a white blouse, a navy blue suit with a light blue blouse, or a lighter grey suit with a dark blue blouse. Shoes should be a dark color, plain pump.

4. Hair for both men and women should be styled in a conservative manner.

5. Mustaches should be neatly trimmed. No handlebars or off-the-wall styles. Facial hair may be questionable in some firms.

6. Make-up and perfume should not be overpowering. They should be used moderately.

7. Jewelry should be limited to watches and wedding bands.

8. Nails should be clean and neatly trimmed.

9. Make sure your teeth are clean, and use a mouthwash or have some breath mints available. There is nothing worse than armadillo breath at an interview.

Dress plays a key role in the way you are perceived. I must again emphasize the importance of looking like a million bucks when interviewing. I strongly recommend men and women purchase one of John Molloy's books. His firm can also prepare a personalized Dress for Success Profile. If a brief questionnaire is completed at the end of his book, he will produce an individualized wardrobe profile for you. This type of service pays for itself many times over the initial investment.

A brief footnote on dressing for success. A number of people ask if you can overdress on an interview? My response is simply, NO! A person is accepted for an interview in a three piece suit in the middle of August in Phoenix, Arizona. On the other hand, if that same person shows up wearing a pair of slacks and a sports shirt, a first good impression is minimized, even if that is the standard of dress for employees.

CAUTION

SWINGING DOOR!

In addition to dressing for success, note that some managers turn down a candidate because of a weight problem. There is still a significant amount of prejudice against obese people. This may not be right, but it happens. If you have put on a few pounds, consider an exercise and diet program. Always check with your doctor before you start any program.

Right & Wrong Turns ... or Interview Do's & Don'ts

Knocking on Heaven's Door.
Mama take this badge off of me.
I can't use it anymore.
It's getting dark, too dark for me too see.
I feel like I'm knocking on Heaven's Door.
Knock, knock, knocking on Heaven's Door.

—BOB DYLAN

Before discussing questions you will be asked during an interview, I have prepared a list of the more important do's and don'ts that should be reviewed prior to the actual interview.

1. Get a good eight hours sleep the night before the interview. You want to appear especially energetic and alert.

2. Do not get caught in the trap of discussing controversial issues. If you find yourself in that position, take a middle-of-the-road stance on the topic.

3. Project a positive, self-assured image, but don't be over-confident. Overstating claims of what you can do for the company are viewed skeptically.

4. Do not offer negative aspects of previous work history. If it comes up, play this down as much as possible and move on to other elements of your career.

5. Never talk unfavorably about your previous boss. Put the bitter feelings aside. Nobody wants to listen to a complainer. Always talk up the positive aspects.

6. Speak highly about the firm at which you are interviewing. Mention achievements noted in the press about the company's products, service, or management.

7. Do not lie! To stretch the truth is one thing, but a deliberate lie to cover up something may someday jeopardize your future.

8. Verbalize responses in a clear, concise manner. Speak in a normal tone, at your own pace.

9. Stress major achievements. Emphasize the positive impact of previous efforts and how you can make similar contributions in the new position.

10. Ask the interviewer if he/she would mind if you took notes during the interview. In addition to collecting valuable information from the discussion, it projects an image of a well-organized person.

11. Interject key questions throughout the interview. Do not wait until the end of the interview. Time may run out and you might lose the opportunity.

12. When you sense the interview coming to a close, use this as an opportunity to re-emphasize interest in the position and how an immediate contribution can be made in the job. Ask when you can expect to hear from them concerning an offer. Although it may seem a little aggressive, try to find out where you stand in the eyes of the interviewer. This gives some indication on how to structure your follow-up activities.

Remember, we all learn by our mistakes. You are not going to come across perfect the first time, but by intensive review and practice, you should be significantly more prepared to respond to the questioning tactics used by the interviewer.

You Are What You Meet ... or The Arrival

Personality has the power to open many doors, but character must keep them open.

—ANON.

Everything presented up to this point is anti-climatic when compared to the actual interview. Although the information gained in the previous section is important, preparation for the interview is far from complete. The following information when applied properly, will open several of the remaining doors and is intended to "key" you up for an interview.

1. Upon arrival for the interview, find a restroom and do a quick final inspection. Make sure everything looks A-OK. Remember to dress for success! Tell the receptionist you have an appointment to see _______________. If the receptionist asks that an application be completed, accept it and inform him/her it will be filled out at home and returned at a later date. Do not fill out an application form in the lobby when there is insufficient time to adequately complete it. After all the time in developing outstanding materials, a hastily filled out application can tarnish well-prepared efforts.

2. If faced with a wait of 30 minutes or more, tell the receptionist that you want to re-schedule the interview at a more convenient time. Leave, don't wait around any longer. Nervousness and tension may set in and can throw off an entire presentation. By taking this action the interviewer is placed on the defensive and will be very apologetic when calling back to re-schedule the interview.

3. If the interview is on time, greet the person with a firm handshake and look him/her directly in the eyes. The first five seconds of direct eye contact is extremely important. It conveys a warm, friendly, open attitude. As you walk to the office, try to start a brief conversation to break the ice. Comment on the appearance of the building or something that you have previously talked about during a telephone conversation. According to Robert Half International, a major recruitment firm, 62% of interviewers make up their mind about a candidate in the first fifteen minutes of the interview. Someone once said, "No one has ever found

a successful way of getting a second chance at making a first good impression."

4. In the office, position yourself as close as possible to the interviewer. Do not sit on one side of the room, if the interviewer is on the other.

5. Be aware of body language as previously discussed.

Gearing Up ... or Survival Questions

There is no answer to a question never asked.

—LAVERNE AND SHIRLEY

OK, so the homework is done. You know how to groom and dress and think it is time to tackle the world. Well, not quite! The final phase to prepare for the interview is the ability to answer some very tough questions.

Most questions asked by the interviewer start with: Who; What; When; Where; Why; and How. These are called "open-ended questions." They should not be answered with a yes or no. The interviewer's job is to obtain information. Normally, they speak 20% of the time and listen the remaining 80%.

Answer questions in a concise, detailed manner. Talk about the specific accomplishments outlined on your resume. Be self-assured, convincing, and express ideas logically. Expound on the value you can bring to the firm. It is extremely important that the interviewer knows from your responses the immediate contributions you can make in the job. Listen very carefully and do not jump right in with an answer. If you are not sure of the question, ask for clarification. When finished with a response, wait for the next question, even if that dreaded pause or silence is intimidating.

There is no need to give more information until asked. If the answer to a specific question is not known, explain without making excuses. Interject questions of your own, prepared from prior research.

A list of sample questions are grouped below according to the type of information an interviewer analyzes. Undoubtedly, you will be asked the same or some variation. I recommend each be studied. Since every person's situation is unique, with different career goals and objectives, it would be impossible to provide standard answers. However, I have tried to answer all in a generic manner that can be modified to fit the situation. Practice answering aloud and perhaps record them using a tape recorder or video camera. Have your spouse or a close friend help. Play back the tape and evaluate it.

PDQ SAMPLE QUESTIONS AND RESPONSES

> *The real art of conversation is not only to say the right thing in the right place, but to leave unsaid the wrong thing at the tempting moment.*
>
> –DOROTHY NEVAL
> Under Five Reigns

I. APPLICANT SELF-PERCEPTION

A. How would you describe yourself?

Always stress positives. You might say, "I am a very loyal and dedicated employee. I am ambitious, set realistic and attainable goals, communicate well, and have the ability to motivate a team of subordinates. I have gained the respect of my peers and subordinates as an effective leader."

B. What are your greatest strengths and weaknesses?

Present your strengths first. Your statement should be an expansion of the answer given to question I.A. above. There is better than a 50% chance that the interviewer will ask a supplemental question related to your strength, and may forget weaknesses. The following would be a typical response: "I do not have any major weaknesses that have a negative impact on my work performance. I continually attempt to sharpen my skills to avoid such problems."

C. In what areas do you feel you need to improve? What self development plans do you have?

This is another way of asking you about weaknesses. Never reveal any major deficiencies. A good explanation would be: "I am continually improving my ability to manage time effectively. Recently, I attended a seminar on time management. By implementing the techniques learned there, I have increased my productivity significantly." Notice how a potential negative was turned into a positive.

D. What are some of the things that motivate you?

"I am motivated by having the opportunity to utilize my talents and experiences to the fullest. I seek an association with a company that encourages innovation and creativity."

E. What do your peers and subordinates think of you?

You could respond with, "My peers constantly seek me out for advice on various subjects. They value my opinion and judgement." Give a personal example.

F. Do you have the qualities to be successful? What are they?

A manager might answer, "During my career I have assumed positions of increasing responsibility. My ability to review situations, evaluate alternatives and make accurate decisions has enabled my career to advance rather quickly." Once again, notice the positive response.

II. WORK EXPERIENCE

A. One of the things we want to talk about today is your work experience. Tell me about your present position?

Here, you want to give details about your current position. Provide specific facts that demonstrate positive results. For example: "As accounting manager I have 30 employees under my supervision. By creating a team effort during the last slowdown in the economy, we were able to reduce our receivables by 20 days, increasing cash flow and reducing interest costs to the company."

B. What are your major responsibilities in your current position?

Develop a variation of the response to question II. A.

C. In what areas do you spend most of your time? Describe a typical day.

Be specific and stress the positive, not the negative time wasters.

D. What are some areas in which you feel you've done particularly well? Why do you feel that way?

You should respond, "Last year our company had a major project that was behind schedule. I was asked to take over the project and bring it back on line. By providing the appropriate leadership, my team rose to the occasion and brought the project to completion 20 days ahead of schedule."

E. Do you have any supervisory experience? Do you consider yourself a successful supervisor? Why?

Again, give specific facts. Call upon your track record of successes.

III. ATTITUDES TOWARDS YOUR JOB

A. What are some of the major problems encountered in your job? What frustrates you the most? What do you do about it?

Here, the interviewer is attempting to find out what upsets you, and how you overcome the problems. A typical reply is: "Dealing with incompetent people gives me much concern. I use my collective skills and abilities to work through the situation. If they are my subordinates, I work with them to identify the problems and take corrective steps such as training or counseling." Always portray a positive mental attitude.

B. In what way has your present job helped develop you to take on even greater responsibilities?

Describe the progression of increased responsibility in your current job. Be very specific: "I started as a sales person with a budget of $500,000 my first year. I exceeded budget by 40%. A promotion to regional manager came two years later. In that capacity I had five sales people working for me and we exceeded our budget by

20%. My track record of success has prepared me for your area sale's position."

C. What are some of the reasons for leaving your last job? Why are you considering leaving your current position?

Every reason for leaving a job should be viewed as positive. For example, you could respond, "In my current position, the opportunities for further growth and development are limited. I am looking for a company where I can apply my talents in a more productive manner."

D. Most jobs have pluses and minuses. What were they in your last or current position?

Identify experiences that added to your professional growth and development. For example, "My present employer selected me to attend the in-house management institute where I received ten months of managerial training." Minuses should be downplayed. Negative responses may indicate a disgruntled employee.

E. Do you consider your progress on the job representative of your ability?

A typical answer could be, "My results speak for themselves. I have made steady progress with my current employer. Unfortunately at this time, my ability to contribute has outpaced the current opportunities."

F. How many hours a week do you feel a person should devote to their job?

The standard answer is: "As many as it takes to perform the job in a commendable manner."

IV. ATTITUDES TOWARDS OTHER EMPLOYEES

A. What type of person would you prefer to have as your manager? Why?

Potential employers like to hear, "I prefer a manager who will give me the opportunity to utilize my skills and experiences to the fullest. Naturally, I would expect guidance and direction as appropriate. A manager must set the climate for the development of teamwork and mutual respect."

B. What are some of the subjects that you and your past managers have disagreed on?

Naturally, every person has disagreed with their boss at some time. Downplay any major problems encountered. Mention situations when you learned from your boss. Give an example.

C. What were some things your boss did that you particularly liked or disliked?

Stress the positive and never speak badly about the boss.

D. How do you feel about the way your supervisor rated your performance?

You might say, "My supervisor was very accurate in his/her assessment of my performance. I learned much from that experience and it will have a positive impact on my future career."

E. In what areas do you feel your supervisor could have done a better job?

Do not be overly critical of your boss, it will only hurt you in the long run. For example, you could state, "He did a very good job, however, I would have liked the opportunity to learn more about certain aspects of our department." This kind of statement is very vague and neutral – therefore, it won't get you into trouble.

F. With what kind of people do you like to be associated? Why?

How about, "I like creative, energetic, responsible people who take pride and ownership in whatever they do. They are the ones who breed success."

V. JOB OBJECTIVES

A. What do you want from your next job that you are not getting from your present one?

This is a very individualized question. A common response would be: "I am seeking greater responsibility. The opportunity to make a company successful and share in the financial rewards that success brings."

B. What are your overall career goals? What plans have you made to achieve these goals?

This is also an individualized question, however, you should set realistic and attainable goals. Don't shoot for the moon, maybe only halfway. If you are too unrealistic, the interviewer may get the feeling that the company cannot offer you an opportunity to attain your objectives.

C. Where would you like to see yourself in two years? Ten years?

Short-term goals should be obtainable with the company you seek employment. Consider the answer, "I am confident that once I start with your company, I will progress to a section management position within two to three years. In ten years, I plan to assume an even greater level of responsibility in the company as a member of the senior management team."

D. What are some of the things you would want to avoid in a job? Why?

Normally, you should offer, "I seek a company that allows a person the opportunity to grow both professionally and personally. Anything less, would be unacceptable."

VI. SALARY

A. What is your salary requirement?

Do not just give out a number. Try to find out the salary range for the position and use the mid-point as the appropriate place to start. Your current employer probably has a similar position and it should not be very difficult to find out the current pay range. If the interviewer indicates a dollar figure that is close to what you had in mind, acknowledge that it is within the range under consideration.

B. What is the least the you would accept to join our firm?

Try to turn the question around to find what the company will pay. If you find yourself in a position where a numerical response is necessary, give a percentage increase rather than a dollar amount. 15 to 20% increases are common, however, don't sell yourself short. I have seen 25 to 50% increases resulting from the perceived value that the person brings to the company.

Once More with Feeling ... or Follow up

Nothing great was ever achieved without enthusiasm.

—RALPH WALDO EMERSON

After returning home from the interview, do an evaluation. Ask yourself questions about various points made throughout this book. How did you do? Did you cover all the points you anticipated? Did you close properly? This self analysis helps you prepare for the next opportunity and your follow-up letter.

The follow-up letter is one of the most useful tools in the PDQ bag of tricks to bring yourself back into focus to the interviewer. It should be typed (hand written only if you have exceptional penmanship) on personal stationery and be one page long. Express your thanks and convey interest in securing an offer for the job. A sample follow-up letter may read like the one shown on the next page:

Follow-up Letter Example

Dear _____:

I would like to take this opportunity to thank you for the time we had on Friday to discuss (company name)'s need for a (position title).

After assessing our meeting, I am confident that I can make an immediate contribution in the position. As previously mentioned, I have made significant achievements in my career that directly relate to the current needs that exist in your firm.

A few of my accomplishments include:

1.

2.

3.

4.

If further clarification is needed, I will be glad to exchange ideas with you. I have a continued interest in the position and I know that our association will be mutually beneficial. I look forward to further discussions.

Sincerely yours,

Tricia Jones

Another PDQ technique previously discussed that makes an impression is to send the follow-up letter via mailgram. Just call your local Western Union operator and dictate the letter. But whether you send a letter or mailgram, make sure to telephone the person in several days. Emphasize a continued interest in the job and inquire when an offer can be expected. If there is a stall tactic, tell them that you are evaluating all alternatives at this time and would like to make a final decision shortly. If you are in the running for the job, this precludes the company from continuing to look for the "ideal" candidate. They would not want to lose you for the sake of an additional week or two of recruitment.

CAUTION

SWINGING DOOR!

Be prepared for rejection. Don't expect a job offer from every company at which you interview, their profile requirements just might not fit. If rejected, use it as a learning experience. Call the interviewer and ask for the reason why an offer was not made. Demonstrate sincerity and explain that you would like to be aware of any shortcomings that may have been a factor. Make adjustments as needed, maintain a positive attitude, and keep the momentum going.

The material discussed on interviews may seem a bit overwhelming, if this is your first job search. However, with consistent application of the PDQ principles outlined, you will become adept when it comes to an interview situation. After several interviews, you should quickly begin to adjust your style to fit the format established by the interviewer and project the image the company seeks.

Revolving Doors ... A Review

Before you go on the interview, research the company and remember to review the "Do's & Don'ts" of interviews. And of course, don't forget body language and how to dress correctly!

Be sure to prepare, using the sample questions presented. Going to an interview unprepared will only lead to a self-fulfilling prophesy, failure. As you answer the questions, remember the concept of "value added." In formulating your responses always interject information that demonstrates your ability to bring something of value to the prospective employer. The interviewer wants to be assured that he/she is getting the best return on their investment. You must convince them that hiring you will bring that return.

Knowing how to respond to questions during an interview is one of the major factors that determines success or failure in job hunting. Update the questions and your responses as you gain experience in the interview process. This is an area where you shouldn't take shortcuts. Practice makes perfect!

DOOR 7

NEGOTIATION

Let's Make a Deal

Comp and Circumstance ... or
Compensation Programs

Follow the Yellow Brick Road ... or
Salary & Bonus

Coffee and Other Perks ... or
Contracts & Fringe Benefits

Off the Beaten Path ... or
Relocation Negotiations

DOOR 7

NEGOTIATION
Let's Make a Deal

The world is governed more by appearances than by realities, so that it is fully as necessary to seem to know something as it is to know it.

—DANIEL WEBSTER

By now, you probably have been on several interviews with some very attractive companies. You know there is interest on their part because a second, and possibly third interview has taken place. The question that should come to mind is, "How do I negotiate the best package?" By the time this section is completed, you should have a high degree of confidence in answering that question.

Comp and Circumstance ... or Compensation Programs

Aim at the sun, and you may not reach it; but your arrow will fly higher than if aimed at an object on a level with yourself.

—J. HAWES

It would be almost impossible for a mechanic to rebuild an automobile engine without first knowing the basic principles of how the engine operates. The same holds true with salary negotiations. You must understand the elements that make up compensation programs before you can effectively negotiate the best package.

Most companies have formalized job descriptions and salary ranges established for each position. Compensation analysts in these companies constantly review job content and conduct or participate in semi-annual salary surveys. They analyze similar jobs in their respective industry and formulate the salary range structure.

Over the years, I have generally structured the salary range of the company's various positions with a 50% spread from the minimum of the range to the maximum. The mid-point number represents the going rate for the fully qualified person in that job category. The following is an example of this:

Minimum	Mid-point	Maximum
$32,000	$40,000	$48,000

Individuals hired low in the salary range traditionally receive more frequent salary reviews than a person at the upper limit. This stems from the theory that the person hired low in the salary range (due to limited experience) learns the elements of the job at a faster rate. When that person becomes fully trained and demonstrates competence in the job, the salary should equate closely to the mid-point of the salary range. After reaching this mid-point, performance reviews are normally given on an annual basis with increases based on merit.

It is important to understand salary guidelines. While this is a simplified explanation of the performance and salary review process, it provides basic knowledge that is essential in order to effectively negotiate. Being brought into a firm at the 90th percentile of the salary range, severely limits the amount of a salary increase when review time rolls around. On the other hand, with a current salary of $32,000 and the mid-point of the salary range $40,000, expect and negotiate an offer close to the mid-point figure. The final salary should not be significantly below mid-point. The acceptance of a salary below mid-point allows for more frequent reviews and salary adjustments. Make sure this is discussed.

Have any agreement on salary review timing put in writing so there are no misunderstandings. The person making the deal may not be there when it's time for your next review.

The more senior position being pursued in a company, the more leeway there is in salary negotiations. At the executive level, the added value an individual brings to a company is of prime importance when making a hiring decision. If a senior-level applicant can make an immediate, significant contribution, exceptions are often made to salary guidelines. I recall one offer to a candidate that put her above the salary range. The value that the individual would bring to the organization was paramount in the decision to hire. The extra dollars it took to bring her on board was outweighed by the individual's potential impact on the bottom line. By the way, I re-evaluated the job, which resulted in a substantial increase in the salary range.

Follow the Yellow Brick Road ... or Salary & Bonus

For every action there is an equal and opposite reaction. If you want to receive a great deal, you first have to give a great deal. If each individual will give of himself to whomever he can, wherever he can, in any way that he can, in the long run he will be compensated in the exact proportion that he gives.

—R. A. HAYWARD

Avoid revealing your current salary until there is enough information about the salary structure of the job. If you plan to "fib" about your current level of salary, keep in mind that the company can easily verify the exact salary. Although it is doubtful that salary would be verified for jobs below $50,000, the company may ask to see a pay stub, W-2 form, or income tax return. They may even ask you to sign a letter permitting previous employers to provide your salary information to the new firm. Honesty is always the best policy.

Key Point

Do not put a number in the answer to salary expectations. Inform the person that you are evaluating all current options and will choose the company offering the best opportunity for professional and financial growth. This is not a cop out, but rather a means that forces the interviewer to carefully examine the pending offer. If there is interest, they are not going to risk the chance of losing you to a competitor for a few dollars. SELL,SELL,SELL the added value that you can bring to the company. Value means more money to you!

If your current salary is relatively low in view of your experience, do not bring this information to the bargaining table too early as it will only be a disadvantage. On the other hand, if you have a high salary, this sends a clear signal to the interviewer that you have achieved a level of success with your current firm.

Most people have a salary number in mind that is acceptable. However, acceptable is not good enough. Setting a higher salary expectation is a must. Higher expectations result in higher salary offers and vice versa. As a rule of thumb, look for an increase of 15 to 20%. Depending on that good old economic theory of supply and demand, offers can be substantially higher than average. Do not underestimate your value, go for the green! Remember, it is all negotiable.

Bonus negotiations should not be forgotten. Almost all companies give some type of bonus to selected employees. Naturally, the more responsibility and impact on the bottom line one has, the greater the rewards. When negotiating a bonus, use these figures as a general rule:

Base Salary	Bonus %
$30,000	5-10
$50,000	10-15
$70,000	15-20
$90,000	20-30
$99,000 +	30-45

Although these are broad guidelines, they provide a good indication of the amount of bonus that can be negotiated. Keep in mind that compensation personnel develop very elaborate bonus plans with numerous variables. Criteria such as return on investment for the CEO to meeting the sales forecast for the Area Sales Manager are utilized in determining bonus plans. Be prepared to discuss the details when the topic surfaces. Utilize past experiences to formulate a bonus program at a new company.

Coffee and Other Perks ... or Contracts & Fringe Benefits

A man's treatment of money is the most decisive test of his character – how he makes it and how he spends it.

–JAMES MOFFAT

After you have negotiated acceptable salary and bonus figures, let the company know they are within your targeted area and move on to other items that need to be in the offer package.

When there is an expectation to make over $60,000 annually in salary and be in a highly visible position, one may want to consider asking for an employment contract. A contract is very specific regarding the terms and conditions of employment and should not be viewed lightly.

Key Point The employment contract provides protection should an unfavorable situation arise, such as a possible merger, acquisition, or start-up. Consult with a reputable lawyer experienced in drafting these contracts. The investment will be paid back with interest should you have to use the protection provisions.

If there is significant resistance to an employment contract, consider a termination clause in the offer letter. Have the company put in a severance pay clause, outlining money and benefits that will be given due to an involuntary termination. Depending on the level of the position, negotiate for a minimum of 3 to 6 months of severance pay. This is common practice in large companies for senior-level employees, but may be obtained from a small organization. It's a give and take situation.

Negotiate further if the severance provision is not offered. For example, under the benefits law, "Cobra," a company must provide an option to continue health insurance coverage after job separation. Although there are specific provisions that apply, the employer is required to inform you of the options. They can make the ex-employee pay up to 102% of the premium cost to continue coverage after termination. Use this information as a negotiable item in a termination agreement. If they will not give extended severance, ask them for six months of insurance premiums instead of you paying 102% of the cost under the "Cobra" law. This could be as much as $300 per month for family coverage.

Key Point

Do not give a current employer notice until you receive the signed offer letter with all details outlined. If something is not right, contact the company immediately and correct the item(s) in question. Have them send out an amended letter. Once the revised offer is RECEIVED, a resignation can be given to your employer.

Many other items should be negotiated depending on your situation. Although it is unrealistic to discuss each in detail, an awareness of the following list enhances one's ability to add to the total compensation package.

ADDITIONAL NEGOTIATION ITEMS

- Company car
- Legal service
- Company loan
- Medical insurance
- Life insurance
- Disability insurance
- Travel accident insurance
- Educational assistance
- Scholarships for children
- Country club membership
- Expense account
- Profit sharing plan

- Retirement plan
- Matching contribution plan
- ESOP — Employee Stock Ownership Plan
- Stock purchase plan
- 401K — Pretax Retirement Plan
- Vacation
- Annual physical examination
- Luncheon club membership
- Sport club membership
- Financial planning
- Relocation assistance

This isn't quite what I had in mind when we were negotiating your "Charge" Account, Mr. Stein!

A Double Take Cartoon

Off the Beaten Path ... or Relocation Negotiations

He who chooses the beginning of a road, also chooses its destination.

—ANON.

Relocation assistance, mentioned on the previous list, is important enough to warrant specific discussion. Assuming you are in the final negotiations of a job offer, relocation assistance can be a significant benefit.

Ask about a home purchase plan. Although very expensive, this kind of program is provided by most major companies. It is more productive to have the new employee and family settled as soon as possible. They do not want the new employee working at the job while the family may be hundreds of miles away. This creates more stress and less productivity.

If the company does not have a home purchase program, find out how much of the home selling expense they are willing to absorb. Try to have them pay all associated costs of selling your residence. Remember, you did a good job in convincing them to hire you and a few more dollars spent on relocation should not pose a major problem.

Also negotiate for the company to pick up costs associated with purchasing a home at the new job location. If interest rates are high, negotiate for mortgage rate differential. What about an introduction to the company's banker and a discounted loan rate or lower points? Everything is negotiable!

Key Point

Be sure to ask for at least two house-hunting trips. Your spouse needs to see the new community before a final decision is made on acceptance or rejection of a job offer. A spouse that is unhappy about the potential location has a significant impact on the decision to move.

To help with the problems of not knowing about a new area, most nationwide real estate firms have relocation assistance programs. They can assign a person to help during the house-hunting trips. An extensive review will be made of individual housing, schooling, and social needs. These firms steer the client in the direction that best fits specific requirements. Check with the real estate firm selling your current residence. They probably have such a program and the cost is zero!

You may have to temporarily leave the family behind to sell the current home. Negotiate for weekend trips home paid by the company. A trip home every third or fourth weekend is not unreasonable. If placed in a situation where you have to live at a new location while your family remains behind for a period of time, make sure the new company pays for living expenses until the move into your new house.

When the time comes to make the actual move, be sure a national moving company is provided. Most hiring companies have standard insurance, which is the depreciation type. If any damage occurs, you will be in for a big shock to find out that only a portion of the value for the item damaged is recoverable.

Key Point

Insist on full replacement insurance when negotiating the moving of household goods. If there is full replacement insurance and an item cannot be repaired, it will be replaced. This coverage saves a lot of headaches and is not that expensive for the company.

Negotiate a relocation sign-up bonus to help defray the costs of a number of hidden moving expenses. For example, the telephone, gas, and electric companies usually require deposits to hook up utilities. Obtaining new license plates for the family cars should be done immediately.

After arrival in the new area, try to wait several months before purchasing a new home. Even if the real estate company has done a good job in presenting the facts about the area, some of the best recommendations can come from new co-workers. They know the area like a book and may give excellent advise.

CAUTION

SWINGING DOOR!

Check with the new company to see how they handle reimbursements of relocation expenses. Make sure they have a gross-up policy. This is where your taxable moving expenses are paid by the company on items that are considered income, but are not deductible on your income tax return. Ask for a copy of the policy. If there is no policy, put everything in writing and consult with an accountant or a local CPA office.

Professional assistance may be needed to handle taxes. There are significant financial implications regarding year-end income tax calculations after moving. If the new company gives you money directly or pays relocation-related bills indirectly, it is considered taxable income. Many items have a dollar for dollar write-off, others do not. You must keep records and receipts of every dollar spent that relates to the move. A list of items should include:

- House-hunting expenses

  Transportation
  Meals
  Lodging

- Current home selling expenses

  Real estate fees
  Attorney fees
  Prepayment penalties
  Points
  Title search fees
  Documentation costs
  Filing fees
  Inspection fees

- Cost of purchasing a new home

  Loan fees
  Attorney fees
  Inspection fees

- Temporary living expenses

  Transportation costs
  Meals
  Lodging

Revolving Doors ... A Review

As you can see, negotiation is a complicated process. Negotiating for financial assistance and relocation shifts the burden to the new company, resulting in a smooth transition for you and the family. Use all of your ammunition to get the best financial package possible. Sell yourself and negotiate for salary, perks, and bonus programs. When all items have been negotiated to your satisfaction, be sure everything is in writing.

CLOSING THE DOOR

Out Of The Maze

CLOSING THE DOOR

OUT OF THE MAZE

Give me your tired, your poor,
Your huddled masses yearning to breathe free,
The wretched refuse of your teaming shore.
Send these, the homeless, tempest - tost to me,
I lift my lamp beside the Golden Door.

—EMMA LAZARUS
Welcome sign on Statue Of Liberty
From the poem The New Colossus

The PDQ system presented in this book should help you find your way to a new job. As stated in the preface, it is not my intention to make you an expert in any one area. Rather, I wanted to provide you a quick way to have enough information about the job hunting process to gain a substantial competitive advantage over the average job seeker. If the various steps outlined in my PDQ system are followed, you should be able to proceed through the employment maze and be on the right path towards a new job. The following is a summary of the information contained in the book.

PDQ Directions to a New Job

Each man's life represents a road toward himself, an attempt at such a road, the intimation of a path. No man has ever been entirely and completely himself. Yet each one strives to become that—one in an awkward, the other in a more intelligent way, each as best he can ... all of us come in at the same door. But each of us ... strives toward his own destiny. We can understand one another; but each of us is able to interpret himself to himself alone.

—HERMANN HESSE
From the book Demian

1. CONDUCT A SELF-EVALUATION AND SET LIFE GOALS – Answer the following questions: Why am I thinking about changing my job? Who am I? Where am I going? What do I want out of life? What makes me happy? What frustrates me? What will really satisfy me? After completing the self evaluation, start to think about setting several life goals. Write them down. Are they realistic? Can they be attained in the time frame established?

2. EVALUATE ALTERNATIVES – After the goals are established, review the alternatives that come into play in order to achieve them. If you are an entrepreneur at heart, will goals be achievable in the current job or working for someone else? Will it be necessary to move into another industry to attain the goals? What about starting your own business? Discuss goals and various courses of action as viewed by your spouse. What is the impact on the family?

3. PLAN YOUR STRATEGY – Develop a strategic marketing plan. Should an executive search firm be used? Is using the local newspaper want ads sufficient? What time frame is established? Is an immediate move acceptable or can you afford to wait several months? Systematically write down thoughts and you will quickly see a plan come together.

4. CREATE A NETWORK – This is perhaps the most overlooked method in which people find out about jobs. Everyone talks about networks, but hardly anyone really uses them. Make a commitment to develop a network. Your Networkers should be professional associates, friends, neighbors, and even old schoolmates. Don't forget about anyone who might help. Remember trust level is essential.

5. PREPARE – Complete the resume data sheet and select the proper resume format. Either write the resume and cover letters or have a professional firm do it. Remember, written materials must be a reflection of you, 100% First Class. Re-call your Networkers and develop leads on various opportunities. Research companies that are of interest. Obtain the names of the key players in the company. Make a "hit list" of individuals to contact. Prepare written questions about the company to ask when interviewed. Formulate answers to anticipated questions.

6. EXECUTE YOUR PLAN – Review the strategy and materials developed. When satisfied, put the wheels into motion. Start the network moving; contact search firms, employment agencies or outplacement firms; subscribe to local and/or national newspapers; send out letters; and start making those telephone calls. Follow Up, Follow Up, and Follow Up!

7. EVALUATE PROGRESS AND MAKE ADJUSTMENTS – After several weeks have passed in the campaign, evaluate the progress. What are you doing right? Why didn't you get that interview? Did you follow up on mailings properly? Look at everything and be very critical of yourself. This is a learning process and adjustments must be made in order to ensure future success.

8. MAXIMIZE THE INTERVIEWING PROCESS – When the interview is scheduled, review all prepared questions and answers; dress for success; and develop the "VALUE CONCEPT," i.e., the value you bring to the company. Remember your body language and to be assertive, show interest, and then follow up after the interview.

9. NEGOTIATE, NEGOTIATE, AND NEGOTIATE – When the choices have been narrowed down to one or two firms, write down financial requirements. Be honest about current salary and the need for an employment contract or a termination agreement. What about relocation costs? Cost of living differentials? Different state tax rates? How about bonuses, stock options, or deferred compensation? Do not give in too quick, you may short change yourself. On the other hand, do not wait too long, making the company have a feeling of uneasiness. Remember it is a give and take situation, both parties must come away from the negotiations as winners.

10. MAKE A FINAL DECISION – When the negotiations are completed, take a few days to evaluate the offer before providing the company an answer. If something is unclear, call for clarification. Discuss it with your spouse and family. Their input is essential. When everyone is in agreement, give a verbal acceptance of the offer. If currently employed, wait for the formal offer in writing before resigning.

11. BONUS STEP ... GO OUT AND CELEBRATE PDQ! – Congratulations! You have successfully negotiated a path through the employment maze to a new job.

Epilogue

Work! Yikes! That's a four-letter word.

–MAYNARD G. KREBS
Dobie Gillis Show

To the first-time job hunter, do not be overly concerned with the breadth and depth of material presented. Take the time to read through the book a second time. You will quickly become very astute about the entire PDQ process. Follow my recommendations – no matter how simple (or complex) they may sound, they work!

For the individual who has been in the work force for several years or changed jobs several times, this book should have provided you a critical review of job hunting techniques. Look at it as a refresher course. Keep an open mind and you can pick up a few points that will enhance your search efforts. With the implementation of the process outlined, you have definitely provided yourself with a competitive advantage over the average job hunter.

If I have been able to provide insight into the job hunting process with my PDQ techniques, I have attained my goal. Finding a job takes a lot of work, but can be fun and exciting. It is a state of mind. The payoff is well worth the investment.

Once settled in your new job, drop me a note on any particular "tricks" or techniques in my PDQ system that helped in your search.

Write to:

Paul Dombroski
PO Box 47604
Phoenix, AZ 85068

Appendix

State	Newspaper	Circulation	Telephone
Alabama	Birmingham News Post Herald	210,000	205-325-2246
Alaska	Anchorage News	68,400	907-257-4237
Arizona	Phoenix Republic and Gazette	456,200	602-271-8704
	Tucson Citizen	146,300	602-573-4290
Arkansas	Little Rock Arkansas Gazette	179,200	501-371-3994
	Little Rock Arkansas Dem.	153,200	501-378-3469
Calif.	Los Angeles Times	1,350,000	213-629-4411
	San Franc. Exam. & Chron.	706,600	415-777-7360
	San Diego Union Tribune	392,400	619-293-1481
	San Jose Mercury News	308,300	408-920-5318
Colorado	Denver Post	425,500	303-820-1539
Conn.	Hartford Courant	301,900	203-525-2525
Delaware	Wilmington News Journal	130,700	800-235-9100
D.C.	Washington Post	1,079,000	202-334-7657
Florida	Miami Herald	505,300	305-376-2828
	Orlando Sentinel	314,200	800-327-6378
	St.Petersburg Times	350,400	813-893-8278
	Tampa Tribune	284,000	813-272-7578
Georgia	Atlanta Journal Constitution	618,100	404-526-5276
Hawaii	Honolulu Star-Bul. & Adv.	196,200	808-525-7499
Idaho	Boise Idaho Statesman	71,200	208-377-6309
Illinois	Chicago Tribune	1,112,200	312-222-2222
Indiana	Indianapolis Star News	400,200	317-633-1175
Iowa	Des Moines Register	364,800	515-284-8103
Kansas	Wichita Eagle-Beacon	194,000	316-268-6386
Kentucky	Louisville Courier-Journal	321,800	502-582-4377
Louis.	Baton Rouge State-Times Adv.	137,000	504-388-0136
Maine	Portland Telegram	137,300	207-871-7690
Maryland	Baltimore Sun	465,400	301-385-1916
Mass.	Boston Globe	805,200	617-929-1500
Michigan	Detroit Free Press	747,300	313-222-6624
	Detroit News	840,000	313-977-7500
Minn.	Minneapolis Star & Trib.	616,300	612-372-4248
	St. Paul Pioneer Press Dis.	245,600	612-228-5240
Miss.	Jackson Clarion-Ledger	114,200	601-961-7286
Missouri	St. Louis Post Dispatch	511,800	314-622-7130
Montana	Billings Gazette	60,300	406-657-1200

Nebraska	Lincoln Journal & Star	79,200	402-473-7451
Nevada	Las Vegas Review-Journal	133,100	702-383-0326
New Ham.	Concord Monitor	21,500	603-224-5301
New Jer.	Newark Star-Ledger	678,800	201-877-4190
New Mex.	Albuquerque Journal	143,200	505-823-3342
New York	Newsday	667,000	516-454-2460
	Daily News	1,597,800	212-949-2000
	New York Times	1,584,300	212-556-8951
N. Car.	Charlotte Observer	269,500	704-379-6960
	Raleigh News & Observer	78,400	919-829-4600
N. Dak.	Fargo Forum	65,400	701-241-5485
Ohio	Cincinnati Post Enquirer	312,600	513-369-1834
	Cleveland Plain Dealer	552,500	216-344-4166
Oklahoma	Oklahoma City Oklahoman	323,600	405-231-3495
Oregon	Portland Oregonian	402,000	503-221-8490
Penn.	Harrisburg Patriot-News	166,500	717-255-8132
	Pittsburgh Press	560,800	412-263-1188
R.I.	Providence Journal	261,000	401-277-7700
S.C.	Myrtle Beach Sun News	188,000	803-577-7111
S.D.	Sioux Falls Argus Leader	60,500	605-331-2345
Tenn.	Knoxville News-Sentinel	163,200	615-637-4111
	Memphis Commercial Appeal	294,000	901-529-2279
	Nashville Tennessean	255,400	615-254-1031
Texas	Austin American Statesman	202,800	512-445-4050
	Dallas Morning News	530,000	214-977-7940
	Dallas Times Herald	387,000	214-720-6574
	Houston Post	356,500	713-840-6880
Utah	Salt Lake City Tribune	140,000	801-237-2770
Vermont	Burlington Free Press	53,400	802-863-3441
Virginia	Richmond Times-Dispatch	238,600	804-649-6471
Wash.	Seattle Times/Post Int.	494,000	206-464-2567
	Spokane Spokesman-Rev./Chr.	137,100	509-459-5081
W.V.	Charleston Gazette Mail	142,300	304-348-1221
Wisconsin	Green Bay Press-Gazette	76,300	414-435-8361
	Madison Wisc. State Journal	145,300	608-252-6333
	Milwaukee Journal	517,400	414-224-2623
Wyoming	Casper Star-Tribune	40,100	307-266-0558

ORDER FORM

(Orders and inquiries, use this form or copy)

Please send me # ______ copies of The Employment Maze.

I am enclosing $ _________. (Arizona residents add applicable sales tax.)

Send check or money order – no cash or C.O.D.'s please.

Make payable and send to:
Paul Dombroski
PO Box 47604
Phoenix, AZ 85068

Name ____

Title ____

Organization ______________________________________

Address ____

City/State/Zip ______________________________________

Phone (_________) _________________________________

QUANTITY DISCOUNTS

(Prices and availability subject to change without notice.)

1-10 copies	$12.95 + $2.00 per book shipping & handling charges
11-50 copies	$11.95 + $1.50 per book shipping & handling charges
51-99 copies	$10.95 + $1.00 per book shipping & handling charges
100-500 copies	$10.35 + $ .50 per book shipping & handling charges
501-999 copies	$ 9.95 + $ .25 per book shipping & handling charges

Please allow four to six weeks for delivery.

Consulting Services

Human Resources and Employment

Paul Dombroski
PO Box 47604
Phoenix, AZ 85068

Marketing, Publishing, and Management

Double Take Productions, Inc.
PO Box 26027
Phoenix, AZ 85068

ORDER FORM

(Orders and inquiries, use this form or copy)

Please send me # ______ copies of The Employment Maze.

I am enclosing $ _________. (Arizona residents add applicable sales tax.)

Send check or money order – no cash or C.O.D.'s please.

Make payable and send to:
Paul Dombroski
PO Box 47604
Phoenix, AZ 85068

Name ____

Title ____

Organization ____

Address ____

City/State/Zip ____

Phone (_________) ____

QUANTITY DISCOUNTS

(Prices and availability subject to change without notice.)

1-10 copies	$12.95 + $2.00 per book shipping & handling charges
11-50 copies	$11.95 + $1.50 per book shipping & handling charges
51-99 copies	$10.95 + $1.00 per book shipping & handling charges
100-500 copies	$10.35 + $ .50 per book shipping & handling charges
501-999 copies	$ 9.95 + $ .25 per book shipping & handling charges

Please allow four to six weeks for delivery.

Consulting Services

Human Resources and Employment

Paul Dombroski
PO Box 47604
Phoenix, AZ 85068

Marketing, Publishing, and Management

Double Take Productions, Inc.
PO Box 26027
Phoenix, AZ 85068

ORDER FORM

(Orders and inquiries, use this form or copy)

Please send me # ______ copies of The Employment Maze.

I am enclosing $ _________. (Arizona residents add applicable sales tax.)

Send check or money order – no cash or C.O.D.'s please.

Make payable and send to:
Paul Dombroski
PO Box 47604
Phoenix, AZ 85068

Name ____

Title ____

Organization __________________________________

Address ______________________________________

City/State/Zip _________________________________

Phone (_________) _____________________________

QUANTITY DISCOUNTS

(Prices and availability subject to change without notice.)

1-10 copies	$12.95 + $2.00 per book shipping & handling charges
11-50 copies	$11.95 + $1.50 per book shipping & handling charges
51-99 copies	$10.95 + $1.00 per book shipping & handling charges
100-500 copies	$10.35 + $ .50 per book shipping & handling charges
501-999 copies	$ 9.95 + $ .25 per book shipping & handling charges

Please allow four to six weeks for delivery.

Consulting Services

Human Resources and Employment

Paul Dombroski
PO Box 47604
Phoenix, AZ 85068

Marketing, Publishing, and Management

Double Take Productions, Inc.
PO Box 26027
Phoenix, AZ 85068

About the Author & Editors

Paul Dombroski is Vice President of a major electronics firm and has more than twenty years experience in the field of human resources management. After receiving his Bachelor of Science degree in Personnel Management from Arizona State University, he started his climb up the corporate ladder.

Paul spent several years in both the public and private sectors of the business world. He worked his way from an entry-level personnel analyst to Vice President of Human Resources. In 1979, he returned to school and obtained his MBA degree.

He is an active member in the American Society of Personnel Administration, the American Society of Training and Development, and the American Compensation Association.

Paul's publications in human resources include: "The Human Resources Function," Professional Services Management Journal; and "Recruitment in High Tech. Can the Smaller Firms Compete?", Electronics West.

David Hage & Dennis Hage are Marketing and Management Consultants and contributed many of the ideas presented in this book. Their education includes B.S. and Master's Degrees. Dennis and David have held various management positions in the corporate world and have had extensive experience in their consulting firm. Their backgrounds include electronics, business, history, education, and computer science.

They have authored and published many articles; a book entitled The Official Goldbuster Guidebook; and are in the process of writing books on several other subjects. In addition, the twin brothers recorded and produced the first-ever "Treasure Hunt" record entitled Superstition Gold and have appeared on national TV and radio networks. Their work also includes a music video and television commercials.